2.99

ALASKA'S
OCEAN
HIGHWAYS

ALASKA'S
OCEAN
HIGHWAYS

A TRAVEL ADVENTURE
ABOARD NORTHERN FERRIES

PHOTOGRAPHY BY MARK KELLEY   TEXT BY SHERRY SIMPSON

Mark Kelley

EPICENTER PRESS

FAIRBANKS ❖ SEATTLE

A special thanks goes to my wife, Jan, and our two sons,
Gabe and Owen, for giving me the time and support to pursue these photos and
to chase my dreams, and for making all my efforts worthwhile.

To Len Laurance, Taquan Air, Don Clothier, Ketchikan Visitors Bureau,
Steve Pierce, George Reifenstein, Linda Mickle, A. J. Slagle, Paul Johnson,
Wings of Alaska, Karen Hansen, Rusty Staub, Sam Wright, Bruce Kruger,
Craig Sempert, Ann Stenford, Jim Ayers, Ketchikan Auto Rental, Brian Wallace,
Ketchikan Air, The Gilmore Hotel, Kent Sturgis, all of the crew and shore staff who
helped me along the way, and finally to the subjects in my photos, thank you all.

Library of Congress Cataloging-in-Publication Data
  Kelley, Mark.
    Alaska's ocean highways : a travel adventure aboard northern
ferries / photography by Mark Kelley ; text by Sherry Simpson.
      p. cm.
    ISBN 0-945397-30-5 (hardcover) ; $32.95. — ISBN 0-945397-31-3
(softcover) ; $19.95
      1. Alaska—Description and travel. 2. Alaska—Pictorial works.
    3. Ferries-Alaska. 4. Ferries—Alaska—Pictorial works.
    I. Simpson, Sherry. II. Title.
F910.5.K45 1995
917.98'2045—dc20
                                                          94-42520
                                                              CIP

Project Editor: Maureen Williams Zimmerman
Text Editor: Christine Ummel
Proofreader: Delisa Clendenon
Maps: Vikki Leib, Jane Terzis
Cover and text design, typesetting: Elizabeth Watson
Prepress and printing: Color Magic, Inc.
Production and binding: Lincoln & Allen
Production manager: Dick Owsiany

To order single copies of *Alaska's Ocean Highways*, mail $32.95 each for a hardcover edition (Washington residents add $2.70 for sales tax) or $19.95 each for a softbound edition (Washington residents add $1.64) plus $5.00 for shipping to: Epicenter Press, Box 82368, Kenmore Station, Seattle, WA 98028.

Booksellers: Retail discounts are available from our trade distributor, Graphic Arts Center Publishing Co., Box 10306, Portland, OR 97210. Phone 800-452-3032.

PRINTED IN THE UNITED STATES OF AMERICA
First printing, February, 1995
10 9 8 7 6 5 4 3 2 1

Photos: *Page 2: Curious passengers gather near the bow as the M/V Malaspina maneuvers into the dock at Haines on Lutak Inlet. Page 5: Snow-covered mountains in the Tongass National Forest tower over the M/V Matanuska in Taiya Inlet. Pages 6-7: A humpback whale dives in the waters of Icy Strait.*

TRAVELOGUES

A CLOSER LOOK

USEFUL INFORMATION

As the throaty horn of the M/V *Matanuska* resonates through the Bellingham harbor, it's impossible not to feel excitement. The massive blue-and-white ship eases away from the dock. The bow wave hisses and roils. A wind rises. The *Matanuska* is no longer tethered to the continental United States. Already the world has divided into two kinds of people: the shorebound (difficult not to feel a little sorry for them) and the northbound.

For more than a century, fortune-seekers, tourists, adventurers, and returning Alaskans have leaned against the rails of ships headed for the Inside Passage and waved good-bye to the ordinary world receding with the wake. Naturalist John Muir predicted this northward pilgrimage. While making his first Southeast Alaska expedition in 1879, he wrote, "Were the attractions of this north coast but half known, thousands of lovers of nature's beauties would come hither each year. I know of no excursion in any part of our vast country where so much is unfolded in so short a time and at so little cost."

That's the essence of the Alaska Marine Highway System. Long before statehood came in 1959, the territory began developing a maritime transportation service as routine and ordinary as a bus line. The first short link, between Juneau, Haines, and Skagway, has grown into a chain of routes that connect coastal communities in Southeast Alaska, Prince William Sound, Kodiak Island, and along the Alaska Peninsula and Aleutian Chain as far west as Unalaska. The fleet of eight "blue canoes," as many locals fondly refer to them, call at thirty-two ports, including Bellingham and Prince Rupert. The service truly is an official highway system; federal highway funds helped the state build ferries and terminals as the system expanded. Happily, this particular government division operates within a spectacular setting, uniting usefulness and beauty. Anyone who harbors a shred of romance can feel it—every ferry trip up the Inside Passage is a journey of possibility, where so much unfolds in so short a time.

This May sailing begins under auspicious omens. Late afternoon sun warms passengers strolling around the decks. A fat sea lion lolls in the harbor, a bon voyage party of one. On the ferry's cavernous car deck, deckhands have arranged cars, pickup trucks, container vans, and motorcycles into sardinelike ranks. Like immigrants preparing

> "I know of no excursion in any part of our vast country where so much is unfolded in so short a time and at so little cost."

◄ *The M/V* Matanuska *arrives at Bellingham, Washington, southernmost port on the Alaska Marine Highway System.*
▲ *Slowly and methodically, northbound vehicles are loaded at Bellingham for the three-day trip to Skagway.*

Soon-to-be passengers Joey Wharton and his son, Ethan, take a snooze while awaiting their turn to board.

for life in the New World, foot passengers parade aboard lugging backpacks, sleeping bags, coolers, guitars. Some people, clad in shorts and sandals, seem prepared for sunny weather to follow them north, while others, forewarned about the damp climate, carry raincoats. A woman clearly expecting the worst sweats in a fur coat. Behind her, a man sports a T-shirt proclaiming, "On the boat again, I can't wait to get on the boat again."

One of the charms of the ferry system is the way people can fashion their own style of travel from the ship's design. People who prefer beds and bathrooms reserved staterooms months ago. Those who would rather rough it spread sleeping bags over lawn-chairs and across the floor in the open-air solarium. Five dome tents, brightly colored as kites, mushroom on the sun deck. Some people have brought along their own provisions. Others will eat three squares in the cafeteria. Ferries are some-times called "the poor man's cruise," but the view promises to be strictly equal opportunity.

As the *Matanuska* gains speed, the town of Bellingham and the state of Washington slip into a distant blue haze. The ship's wake unspools like a ribbon, and before long passengers gathered at the stern wander forward to the bow. The ship is headed north, and people want to face that direction, to see where they're going. The shadowed coastline glides by, homes giving way to unsettled landscape. People brace themselves against the rails and take deep, rejuvenating breaths of cool, briny air. When the purser announces, "We're on Alaska time now," passengers set their watches back an hour, and their minds ahead to the Inside Passage.

This is how Alaska should be approached—from the sea. Everyone who has ever claimed to discover it—as if a land already

Kite-flying youngsters quickly learn that the stern is the best place to catch the wind on the ferries.

Members of running teams en route to Skagway for the Klondike Trail Relay discuss strategy on a northbound ferry.

peopled by beautiful and complex cultures could be "discovered"—came by sea. Early adventurers searched this raw coast for the Northwest Passage. The *Matanuska's* passengers make their own voyages of discovery as the ship crosses sounds, rounds capes, enters deep inlets. What they see is more than scenery, because scenery implies mere prettiness, a mild-mannered landscape. This is a thousand miles of wild beauty rimming the coast between Bellingham and Skagway, a thousand miles governed by the movement of ocean, the flux of weather, the interplay of mountains and rain forest.

By the second day, when the *Matanuska's* passengers realize the view isn't going anywhere, they relax and watch the British Columbia coast slide by. "I feel like my muscles are melting or something," one passenger confides to another. The ship offers amnesty from the modern world. No telephones, no cable television, no fax machines, no need to be anywhere. Out here, the ship is safe from news. The only information of value is spread by word of mouth: Quick! There's a humpback whale to starboard! Is it raining? Look at that tugboat. When will we reach Ketchikan? What's for dinner?

Some people claim they're going crazy after the first day on board, but that's only because they've forgotten how to entertain themselves. Others have no problem. A woman immerses herself in a novel, her feet in her husband's lap. Oblivious to the passing view, bridge players concentrate on their cards. A young mother crochets, a pool of calm among a whirling brood asking the inevitable question: When are we going to get there? Up in the solarium, young people bask in the sun like sea lions. Two guitar players, a banjo player, and a bongo drummer syncopate into a rock song; nearby listeners applaud when they're done. Down in the bar, a pair of musicians on their way to a gig in Petersburg take requests for Billy Joel songs, but they prefer playing jazz, smooth and resonant, like the boat's passage.

13

One of the charms of traveling on Alaska's ferries is the relaxed atmosphere—no phones, no fax, no hurry.

Mostly, people talk. Alaska's ferries bring together unlikely groups: Mennonites and motorcycle clubs, senior citizens and schoolkids, fishermen and foreigners. Everyone headed to Alaska has a story, and on ferries, people have time to spin out their tales. Some want adventure. Some want peace and quiet. Some are going home. Some are seeking a home. Some have nothing better to do. Some are looking for something better. For many, the ferry ride represents but a leg of a longer journey. For others, it *is* the journey.

An Oregon man leans over the bow to watch the surging bow wake and confesses that this is his first time on a vessel bigger than a rowboat. He spent the last of his money to buy passage to Ketchikan to seek work in a cannery; the thrill of being at sea has temporarily eased his financial worries. Long after most people have sought shelter from the chilly evening wind, he remains out on deck watching his past disappear in the wake.

An older man from the Midwest reveals his true destination: Juneau's Mendenhall Glacier. "I've always dreamed of standing on a glacier," he announces. He plans to disembark, head right to that great big blue hunk of ice, and then fly home.

In the dining room, a middle-aged woman from eastern Washington wears a red bandanna and a slightly stunned look on her face. While attending a professional conference in Seattle, she was overcome by the desire to travel the ferry to Alaska. She caught a shuttle to Bellingham, bought her ticket, and boarded the *Matanuska* wearing a dress and carrying only a credit card. By the time the trip is over, she will have purchased a jacket and hat in the ferry's gift shop, socks in Ketchikan, a camera in Skagway, and sweatpants and binoculars in Sitka.

A lanky Texan named, of course, Tex pulls out his driver's license to prove he is indeed 93 years old. "That's my little honey over there," he says, nodding at his wife Barbara. On this, their eighth trip to Alaska, they'll drive their motorhome off the boat

at Haines, drive a giant loop through Canada and Alaska, and go fishing at Ninilchik on the Kenai Peninsula. From his shirt pocket Tex pulls out worn snapshots of his last catch there—the 72-pound halibut is his. Next time you show these pictures, an Alaskan advises him, claim you caught the 179-pounder.

In the forward lounge, a Tlingit teenager from Kake and a grandmother from Petersburg explain Alaska to a curious Hispanic woman from Seattle. The tourist wants to know which is the best Southeast town to live in. A pause as the Alaskans think it over. "The one I would pick is Sitka," the grandmother finally says. The teenager agrees. "I think it's the prettiest. It's not that big and it's not that small." The grandmother adds, "And it's so peaceful." The woman from Seattle says, "Sitka, eh?" as if she were already making plans to move there.

A fisherman from Craig shepherds his visiting parents on their Alaska tour. In the bar, he offers advice about bears to a nervous young Boston woman who will be camping her way to Homer. He tells her: Don't rub lard all over your body. Don't hang a dead salmon in your tent. In fact, put your tent up a tree.

Then he tells her about the time his purse seiner caught a humpback whale, and how his crew untangled the leviathan from the net. It's an entertaining tale, like most you'll hear on this ship of stories.

Near Bella Bella, B.C., a sturdy tugboat tows a barge laden with freight containers, pickup trucks, and even pleasure boats. As the ferry slides past, the tug crew steps out onto the deck and waves vigorously. There are many such travelers along the Inside Passage.

"I love this passage," says Duncan, an Alaska jack-of-all-trades headed for Ketchikan. He gazes out the window at the

forested shore. "I've been on it several times in boats of all sizes." Asked which boat is the best, he grins crookedly. "The bigger the better." At 408 feet, the *Matanuska* is just about right, he says.

The ocean is everything here. Many people make their living on the water, and still more make their fun there. The straits, channels, and passages that web the Alexander Archipelago are as familiar to seagoing residents as interstate freeways, the inlets and coves as necessary as exit ramps. As the ferry nears a community, waterborne traffic increases as boats of every size and character radiate from port. Fishing boats on their way to catch black cod dip and rock in the ferry's wake. Tugboats tow log rafts of small forests lashed together. Stately cruise ships forsake the Mediterranean, Caribbean, and Mexican seas for the cooler delights of Alaska. On the major channels, timber and freight ships steam for Japan and other overseas markets. Sailboats skim across the water, and sportfishing boats zip past, bound for secret fishing holes. Beachcombers and campers pull their skiffs up on remote beaches. Even six lazy seagulls bum a ride from a driftwood log.

The voyagers who draw the most attention appear suddenly, like a meteor shower. As the ferry steams through Fitz Hugh Sound in the gauzy, golden light of early evening, a gang of Dall porpoises streaks across the channel to frolic in the ship's wake. The porpoises explode through the water, sickle fins slicing through the waves. An especially playful porpoise repeatedly throws itself out of the water onto its back, exposing the black-and-white markings that resemble those of a killer whale. "Woooo! You're beautiful!" shouts a delighted passenger. On the solarium deck, someone blows giant soap bubbles that bob and soar in the breeze before disappearing. The sunny scene is so idyllic that a silver-haired man turns to a perfect stranger and says, "Isn't this a lovely trip?"

Other visions appear. A fleet of Pacific white-sided dolphins arc from the water so quickly they resemble skipping

15

In between whale and bald eagle sightings, passengers soak up sunshine on a glorious day in mid-summer.

rocks. "I know my photos are only going to show little white splashes," says a woman ruefully, but she continues snapping pictures anyway.

It is the whales that cause everyone, even long-time Alaskans, to bolt for the windows and decks. You can almost feel the ship shift slightly. During a movie, an announcement of humpbacks ahead empties the lounge as if someone had shouted "Fire!" In the cafeteria, the only ambience needed is the sudden rolling appearance of a humpback through the stern window.

There are other, quieter beauties. Dramatic features—mountains, glaciers, wildlife—overwhelm the more subtle and meditative aspects of the journey. In a pale dawn, clouds avalanche in slow motion down an island peak. As the day progresses, the color of the sea changes from a pearly gray to a mossy green until, finally, the caramel light of sunset spills across the water. Even rainy days—and there are plenty of them—present a delicate palette of grays. "It's always different, isn't it?" observes a New York woman. "The light comes through the clouds a certain way, or you see a rainbow, and it's all new."

The water is always different, too. Only when the *Matanuska* crosses Queen Charlotte Sound do passengers fully understand how sheltered the Inside Passage is. As the ship emerges from the east side of Vancouver Island into open water, big swells and whitecapped seas sweep in from the Pacific and roll the boat, as well as some stomachs. Occasionally a wave smashes against the hull, clanging it like a bell. Some passengers retreat to their staterooms or sleeping bags, fighting off seasickness. A few brace themselves in the bow, ducking as sea spray flings over the railings. The man who has never been in a boat leans into the wind and grins. "This is the best place to be," he says. After the two-hour crossing, a seaman pronounces the passage through the sound "pretty decent," which makes those listening grateful they experienced only a taste of the ocean's power.

16

Travelers complete the unwinding process when they realize the magnificent scenery isn't going anywhere.

The M/V Columbia rounds Pennock Island soon after departing the waterfront fishing town of Ketchikan.

Early on the second morning, the *Matanuska* crosses Dixon Entrance and the invisible border separating Canada and the United States. Until now, communities appeared only as constellations of light and activity studding the coastline. When the *Matanuska* docks in Ketchikan, its first port of call, people are ready to walk on something that doesn't move under their feet. The ship remains long enough for some to breakfast in a nearby cafe, others to visit a grocery store, and a few fast walkers to trek downtown and back. The town is still waking up, but its rowdy, hardworking character is clear. "It's like border towns anywhere," the fisherman from Craig says. The *Matanuska* resumes its northbound journey in a drizzle, sliding past its berthed sister ship, the *Malaspina*. After undergoing maintenance in drydock, the *Malaspina* will return to service in a couple of weeks.

As the ship docks in Wrangell in the afternoon, everyone's attention is diverted by a cloud of eagles circling and swooping near the waterfront. People lose track after counting thirty. In a cyclone of great wings and talons, the birds dive at spring herring gathered in the bay. A deckhand calls it an "eagles concert." The bartender, who looks as if she has seen everything at one time or another, stops cleaning windows long enough to say, "Isn't that incredible?" After hundreds of trips, even the crew can be surprised now and then.

On shore, local kids appear and form a ragged line to greet disembarking passengers. They are the state's youngest entrepreneurs, hawking garnets gathered from a nearby deposit willed to Wrangell's youth by a local businessman. Over the years, the proceeds have financed everything from bubble gum to bicycles, and even the occasional college education. The cranberry-colored gems are separated by size and quality in muffin tins, tackle boxes, and TV trays. The kids also are varied in size and polish, but all

Overlooking Tongass Narrows, the Cape Fox Lodge is reached by tramway from downtown Ketchikan.

A pair of kayakers explore Ketchikan's historic Creek Street district from water level on a blue-sky day.

Wrangell is a fishing and tourism town on Wrangell Island, at the confluence of Sumner Strait and the Stikine River.

are friendly, polite, and cute, an irresistible combination for many of the visitors who stop to buy a few garnets.

The approach to Petersburg is long and dramatic. The *Matanuska* crosses the Stikine River's silty drainage and enters the Wrangell Narrows, a pipe cleaner of a passage that twists between Kupreanof and Mitkof islands. A seaman watches from the bow for obstacles, boats, and debris in the water as the wheelhouse crew smartly maneuvers the ship according to a string of more than seventy navigational aids and markers along the twenty-one-mile channel. A ship's master once noted that it's one thing to navigate this challenging passage in broad daylight on a good tide. It's a little different in a snowstorm, he said.

The landscape grows intimate as the waterway constricts into a green artery pulsing with the tide. Everyone takes a good, long look at a bald eagle perched on a reef two hundred feet away. "This must be why they call it the Narrows," a passenger says, laughing a trifle nervously. "It's

21

▲ *As a history pole, the Sun Pole in Wrangell represents the story of a particular Native clan.*
▶▲ *On Chief Shakes Island near Wrangell, this Tlingit tribal house is a popular destination for visitors.*

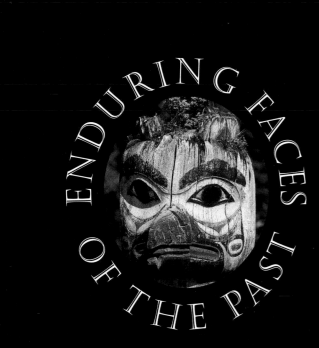

ENDURING FACES OF THE PAST

Evocative, mysterious, and legendary, totems embody not only the individual talents of their carvers but express a way of life.

▲ *The eyes of Raven watch over the grounds of Saxman Totem Park near Ketchikan.* ▶ *Purple lilacs, mountain ash, and red hawthorn surround this Amos Wallace totem pole in Juneau.*

22

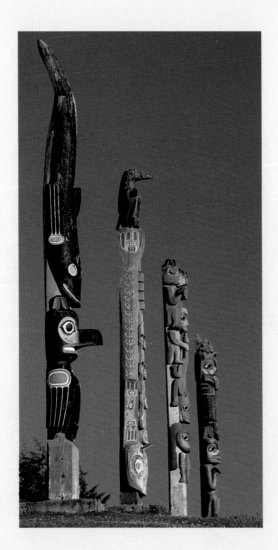

Among Southeast Alaska's most intriguing attractions are totem poles. Evocative, mysterious, and legendary, they embody not only the individual talents of their carvers but express a way of life. As an art form, the totem pole has changed just as Tlingit and Haida cultures have changed after their first contact with Russians, other Europeans, and Americans. Many poles exhibited or displayed in Southeast towns are replicas of ancient poles that have succumbed to time and climate.

Totems are not meant to be "read" but rather interpreted in the context of their various purposes and owners. *Legend poles* represent tales, folklore, or actual experiences worth remembering. Such poles may depict well-known stories, such as Raven bringing the world daylight, displayed in replica in Wrangell's Kiks'adi Totem Park. As charming and entertaining as these legends may seem to casual onlookers, they were highly significant to their creators.

One of the oldest forms, *crest poles* herald family lines. A *history pole*, such as the Sun Pole at Wrangell or the modern Wooshkeetaan pole carved in 1980 in

Juneau, tells about a particular clan. *Memorial poles* were commissioned to honor a certain person; one example is the One-Legged Fisherman pole commemorating the nephew of Chief Shakes VII, which is displayed in replica at Kiks'adi Totem Park. *Mortuary poles* held the remains of a high-ranking dead person. *Shame poles*, such as the Trader Legend replica at Sitka National Historical Park, publicly ridiculed someone for acts of wrongdoing, unpaid debts, and the like.

The significance of many poles has been lost because the stories that inspired the images have disappeared. But even novices can puzzle out the identity of some figures with practice or with the help of interpretive guides. Images might portray mythical beings; creatures from the natural world, such as whales, frogs, bears, or wolves; or figures with supernatural powers, such as the Village Watchman. Other items depicted on poles include ornamental or decorative goods, ceremonial hats, and staffs.

Scores of poles exist throughout Southeast Alaska in museums and totem parks. These include Totem Bight State

A row of brightly painted totem poles stands in Klawock Totem Park on Prince of Wales Island.

many ancient poles recovered from abandoned villages. In addition, beautiful poles stand within several towns. Kake, for example, lies under the gaze of a 132.5-foot pole that is often incorrectly identified as the world's tallest (an honor belonging to a 173-foot pole on Vancouver Island, British Columbia). Nearly a score of totem poles are displayed throughout Juneau.

The wide variety of poles shows what a dynamic art form they are. Poles in the green light of forest bear a different aspect than those in museums. Each pole is strikingly individual.

Today new generations of artisans such as Nathan Jackson, Wayne Price, Jim Marks, George and Mick Beasley, and others are replicating old poles and creating new ones. Modern poles sometimes commemorate local Native groups, such as the Auk Tribe Pole carved by Nathan Jackson in 1981. Displayed at Juneau's Centennial Hall, the pole honors the area's Tlingits by combining symbols and crests that represent Auk clan history. Other poles tie modern history to Native cosmology; such a work is the "Harnessing of the Atom Pole" carved by Juneau artist Amos Wallace. The contemporary and creative nature of totem pole carving reflects the enduring appeal of this art form.

Park at Ketchikan; Saxman Totem Park, near Ketchikan; Sitka National Historical Park; Kiks'adi Totem Park and Shakes Island in Wrangell; and parks in Hydaburg, Kasaan, and Klawock. Ketchikan's Totem Heritage Center houses and displays

Only a few miles from Ketchikan, the totem park in Saxman serves as a testimony to traditional Tlingit culture.

Originally settled as a Norwegian fishing village, Petersburg today has a harbor teeming with commercial fishing boats.

really narrow." New pilots train gradually and carefully for this stretch by learning it piece by piece under the tutelage of an experienced captain.

As the vessel slips past the cabins and houses tucked along the shoreline, some passengers imagine themselves living in these quiet eddies of civilization, where the ferry's appearance might be the biggest event of the day. When the wheelhouse announces a deer on the starboard shore, few people see it, but the knowledge that wildlife is out there triggers a rash of sightings. "There's a bear—there, in the meadow," someone calls out, and virtually everyone in the lounge rushes to see. "There's another one!" someone shouts, and bear fever infects the group.

"Where?"

"There!"

"I don't see anything!"

Confused by dusk's shadows, passengers claim to spot five or six different bears along the forested shore. "I've seen them at the zoo," a man remarks. "I don't know why I'm so excited." Because this isn't a zoo; because this is a place where every glimpse of some wild thing is a moment of grace.

Experienced wildlife viewers keep their counsel; where others imagine bears, only large, bear-like rocks stand in the dusk. But there's no honor in deflating the moment. Bears do walk these shores, after all.

When the *Matanuska* departs Petersburg at midnight, few passengers are awake to hear the ship's horn echoing against the mountains. Through the night, the ferry rumbles north, the powerful engines vibrating in the bones. Night cloaks the flank of Admiralty Island as the ship crosses Frederick Sound and enters Stephens Passage.

27

Three local children pole their makeshift boat down Hammer Slough on Mitkof Island.

In the cottony light of 6:30 a.m., solarium passengers cocooned in their sleeping bags poke their heads out into the cool air and wonder where they are and where they've been. An eagle watches impassively from its treetop perch as the ferry docks at the Auke Bay ferry terminal, thirteen miles northwest of Juneau. Despite the early hour, passengers fan out on mini-excursions. Some take an inexpensive bus tour of downtown Juneau. Others are whisked to the Mendenhall Glacier a few miles away. A chattering crowd of thirty-five youngsters boards the ship for a field trip to Skagway, accompanied by assorted teachers and chaperones. A few passengers exchange long-suffering glances, but the kids quietly settle down with workbooks, cards, and games. As the *Matanuska* reverses away from the dock, people line the decks for a last glimpse of the blue cascade of ice descending from the Juneau Icefield. The man who came to see the Mendenhall Glacier is there now, realizing his dream.

The ship continues on through Lynn Canal, a concentrated stretch of Inside Passage squeezed between the ragged white peaks of the Chilkats to the west and the stolid bulk of the Coast Mountains to the east.

Near Shelter Island, a humpback whale and her calf loft their flukes and dive. "This country gets more beautiful the farther north you go," muses the Craig fisherman.

After lunch, the public address system announces a weekly emergency drill for the crew. Evidently, the excitement is a bit much for some passengers. Ten minutes later, the address system crackles on again with another message: "For the information of passengers, the drill is for crew only." Passengers who have been searching for their lifeboat stations sheepishly return to their seats. When the drill horn blasts, the schoolkids jump up and melodramatically clap their hands over their ears.

The cloud cover blurring the sky dissipates as the ship passes lonely Eldred Rock Lighthouse. By the time the *Matanuska* arrives

◄ *Above the city's twinkling lights, alpenglow illuminates the snowy peaks of Mount Juneau on a winter evening.*
▲ *The Fourth of July in Alaska's capital city is celebrated with an elaborate parade down Front Street.*

◄ *From Brotherhood Park, Mendenhall Glacier looks like a giant sheet of blue ice, slowly sliding into the valley.*
▲ *Backdropped by the Cathedral Peaks, a lone automobile heads towards the Haines ferry dock.*

at Haines, skies are brighter. Up here, where the Panhandle is soldered to the rest of Alaska, the climate dries out a bit. Those admiring the picturesque setting from the deck aren't going anywhere just yet. Inside, everyone else is busy gathering their belongings and preparing for a pilgrimage up the Alaska Highway. Farewells permeate the ship as new friends exchange addresses, good wishes, even hugs. A couple who used to be a lawyer and an estate groundskeeper in a former life pedal their overladen bicycles down the road, wobbling a bit under their loads. Tex and Barbara rumble out of the ship's belly in their motorhome; they have an appointment to keep with a halibut. Members of a Georgia family moving to Fairbanks press their faces against the window of their station wagon, getting used to their new home. The rest of Alaska is that-away.

Lighter and less crowded, the *Matanuska* continues on its last northbound hour the seventeen miles up Taiya Inlet, a tentacle of water reaching toward Canada. In the forward lounge, passengers search the knobby mountains for goats. Stale snow dapples the slopes, competing with the fresh, raw green of newly leaved trees. Before long, a dilemma presents itself: continue counting mountain goats clinging to the rocky bluffs, or dash outside for a glimpse of leaping killer whales? The whales win again.

For passengers, the layover at Skagway is a chance to explore Alaska's most famous gold-rush town. Once a boomtown awash with Klondikers, the town surrenders each spring to hundreds of thousands of tourists who arrive by cruise ship, car, and ferry. This early in the season, disembarking ferry passengers represent the advance troops. Anyone who leaves the ship is exiled to shore for three hours while the crew frantically cleans the ferry during what is called "turn-around." Avalanches of laundry clog the corridors, and vacuum cleaners roar through the lounges. Meanwhile, most of the passengers end up in the Red Onion Saloon, nursing beers and listening to one of their own pound the upright piano.

Skagway, at the head of Taiya Inlet, is the Marine Highway's northernmost destination in Southeast Alaska.

▲ *A vintage locomotive on the White Pass & Yukon Route steams into the gold-rush town of Skagway.*
▶ ▲ *Dressed in clothes from the Klondike days, owner Jan Wrentmore welcomes visitors to Skagway's Red Onion Saloon.*

A LAND SHAPED BY SEA & ICE

To John Muir,
glaciers weren't cold and
lifeless blocks of ice, but living,
beautiful forces creating
new landscapes.

▲ *A harbor seal relaxes in the*
comfort of its icy bed. ▶ *Avalanches of*
ice calve from the frozen face of Sawyer
Glacier in the Tracy Arm-Fords
Terror Wilderness.

34

Water is the key to landscape in Southeast Alaska. At least four times during the past few million years, ice advanced and retreated over most of the Panhandle in a sheet five thousand feet deep in places, grinding mountains and hollowing out deep, U-shaped valleys. Only mountain spires called *nunataks* protruded from the cold blanket that reached out into the Pacific Ocean as far as the continental shelf. As the climate warmed between ten and twelve thousand years ago, the retreat of the Wisconsin ice sheet further gouged out deep valleys, many of which filled with seawater to become fjords. In some parts of Southeast, a recent cooling period called the Little Ice Age again filled valleys with glaciers that have retreated within the past two hundred years. Many are still retreating, and glacial action continues sculpting as new land is exposed, moraine and silt is deposited, and rivers braid across valley floors. Spectacular Ice Age remnants include the fifteen-hundred-square-mile Juneau Icefield, which feeds some three dozen glaciers, including the well-known Mendenhall Glacier.

Under Nugget Glacier near Juneau, one intrepid explorer is immersed in the blue glow of the ice caves.

Not only did retreating ice gouge and scour the landscape, but it freed the land from a stupendous weight, allowing it to rebound. In some areas land continues rising, as much as 1.5 inches annually in places like Glacier Bay. Released from its icy grip over the past two centuries, Glacier Bay also has become a living laboratory for scientists interested in how plants and animals colonize raw landscape.

Frozen water shaped the land, but falling water vegetates it. The warm, moist air of the Pacific Ocean means rain, and lots of it. Prevailing southerly winds, the offshore Japanese Current, and storms raging off the Pacific shove weather systems against the Coast Range fringing the mainland. Rain and snow fall as air stopped by this granite barrier condenses. The mountainous landforms also affect how much rain falls where; Little Port Walter on Baranof Island might receive as much as three hundred inches of precipitation annually, while Haines enjoys a relatively dry thirty-five or so inches each year. Residents of downtown Juneau might receive almost twice as much rain annually as those who live in the Mendenhall Valley, about ten miles away. Mild temperatures and this persistent damp foster the temperate rain forest that covers Southeast

Alaska. Rain also swells the major rivers and countless lesser streams that serve as spawning grounds for chinook, coho, sockeye, chum, and pink salmon.

Nobody appreciated the splendors of

Southeast Alaska more than John Muir, who began studying glaciers in the Sierra Nevada Mountains and came to Alaska in 1879 to confirm his theories. Muir was fascinated by "ancient glaciers and the

37

 A trio of harbor seals floats contentedly on their iceburg in the waters of Tracy Arm.
▶ ▶ *A float plane cruises over the Juneau Icefield, an Ice Age souvenir that covers fifteen hundred square miles.*

influence they exerted in sculpturing the rocks over which they passed with tremendous pressure, making new landscapes, scenery and beauty which so mysteriously influence every human being, and to some extent all life. . . ." To him, glaciers weren't cold and lifeless blocks of ice, but living, beautiful forces. He was probably the first white man to see Glacier Bay, and he returned several times to study the area. Today he is remembered more as a nature writer than a scientist, but his early interest in the region drew the attention of important scientists.

Several dramatic examples of these forces of nature stud the Southeast coastline. Misty Fiords National Monument, a 2.3-million-acre region near Ketchikan, embraces granite cliffs, deep embayments, bold bluffs, and numerous glaciers. Similarly, Tracy Arm, forty-five miles south of Juneau, slices into the coast, jeweled at its head with the twin faces of Sawyer Glacier. Glacier Bay National Park and Preserve, about fifty miles west of Juneau, includes 3.3 million acres of mountains, inlets, wildlife, and glaciers that have become legendary among wilderness enthusiasts. Each of these areas can be toured by charter boats, helicopters, or airplanes. Passengers can see several glaciers between Ketchikan and Skagway.

A trip up Harbor Mountain on Baranof Island provides a spectacular view of downtown Sitka.

Through the night, the *Matanuska* retraces its journey as far as Juneau before heading to Sitka on the outer coast. The ship rounds Admiralty Island to sail down the wide marine thoroughfare of Chatham Strait. On this trip, the ferry bypasses the Tlingit village of Angoon, the island's only permanent community, and turns into Peril Strait. One of the marine highway's main attractions lies at the mouth of the strait, where Sergius Narrows separates Baranof and Chichagof islands. From the wheelhouse a voice explains that the ferry can only transit the narrows at slack tide, when the tidal current is not running.

As the ship threads a passage along a chain of islands and navigational aids, people tense. At one spot, three red buoys lie about three hundred feet offshore, guiding the ship through a channel so skinny that passengers lean forward, then shift to the edge of their seats, and stand up as the ship squeezes through the gap. Sighs of relief wash through the lounge as people realize the ferry wasn't going to brush against the trees after all.

In Salisbury Sound, a few sea otters appear, nonchalantly backpaddling at the ship's approach. Muscular swells from the open ocean heave under the ferry until it enters Neva Strait. Locals and visitors alike venture out into the sunshine and peer into coves and inlets that dimple the coast. Sitka residents point out good fishing spots to a visiting German couple, while an Alaskan bends the ears of two tourists who make the mistake of asking about the local economy.

Once docked at the Sitka terminal, the *Matanuska* waits three hours for the tide to slosh through Sergius Narrows. Most passengers abandon ship for tours of the Russian-American town a few miles to the south. Those who wander north on foot visit the original site of New Archangel, as the settlement was known

The elegant spires atop St. Michael's Cathedral recall Sitka's past as the capital of Russian America.

before Tlingit Indians burned the fort and massacred Russian settlers in 1802. The furies of the bloody past seem far away from the sunny morning. Out on the tidal flats, two men and a boy madly shovel mud in pursuit of wily clams as eagles wheel overhead. In a many-jointed ballet, a pair of great blue herons stalk through an estuary.

As the ship returns to Peril Strait, the officer on watch has a bit of fun with gullible passengers. He announces the approach of Highwater Island, home to the "Siberian flamingo," which he describes as a new migrant to Alaska since the end of the Cold War. Passengers crane their necks to look for these most unusual birds, and finally someone spots them: a flock of pink plastic flamingos roosting permanently in the trees. A North Dakota woman who doesn't get the joke turns to an Alaskan and asks, "Really?" Chalk up another victim of the Siberian flamingo prank.

When the purser announces a comedy will show in the viewing lounge, someone asks, "Why on earth would anybody watch a movie when they can see this go by?" The entertainment value of "this" increases a few notches when humpback whales begin breaching near Fairway Island. Flippers twist in the air and slap the water. A whale heaves into the air and crashes into the water, and excited passengers emit a collective "Ohhh!" Where Peril Strait joins Chatham Strait, a pair of whales breach in tandem. A young German backpacker says to his companion, "Now I've seen everything there is to see," but he's wrong. You can never see everything in the Inside Passage.

As the *Matanuska* makes a wide turn to the south, passengers drift back to their seats. In the distance, the broad backs of the retreating whales gleam in the setting sun. The rest of the journey to Bellingham lies ahead. Tomorrow, more islands will appear. The *Matanuska* will call at other ports. The light will change. It is all the same, and never the same, on the Alaska Marine Highway.

A sea otter floats along on the surface of Cross Sound, carrying its young pup on its chest.

In between Haines and Juneau, a full moon sets over the peaks of the Chilkat Mountains.

SHIPBOARD ARTS & EDUCATION

Elementary school
children love learning about
geography, eagle biology, and
wildlife habitat when they are
taught aboard a ferry.

▲ *A hungry bald eagle snatches up*
44 *a herring snack.* ▶ *A pod of killer*
whales surfaces during its crossing
of Icy Strait.

On a cold November day, about sixty excited students from Juneau's Harborview Elementary School stream aboard the M/V *Matanuska*. On their way to visit the Alaska Chilkat Bald Eagle Preserve in Haines, they'll spend the four-hour cruise studying Southeast geography, eagle biology, and wildlife habitats before riding school buses to the preserve and returning home on their floating classroom. Most of the kids agree that it's the best school day they'll have all year.

Alaska's ferries act as more than comfortable barges or tour ships. They also help entertain and educate passengers. During the summer, interpreters from the Alaska Department of Fish and Game and the U.S. Forest Service ride the mainline ships and help visitors understand what they're seeing. Programs include lectures, movies, displays, and slides on local history, culture, wildlife, and geography. When there's time, interpreters might lead nature walks ashore. They also lend natural history books, display maps, announce passing sights, and, of course, answer questions by the score.

The eagle programs are especially popular. In recent years, the ferry system and the Alaska Department of Fish and Game have offered lectures on bald eagles in November and December, when people travel to see as many as thirty-five hundred eagles gathered to feed on spawning salmon at the Alaska Chilkat Bald Eagle Preserve in Haines.

A special attraction of these programs is a young bald eagle named Buddy, the star of Sitka's Alaska Raptor Rehabilitation Center. The center treats and cares for eagles, owls, falcons, and other raptors; those birds that cannot be returned to the wild remain at the center. Unlike many of the patients, who are recovering from gunshot wounds, collisions, infections, electrocution, and other injuries, Buddy's problem is psychological. Illegally raised from youth by people, he has "imprinted" on humans and has even courted one of his human handlers. His trips on the ferry allow thrilled passengers a chance to meet a friendly member of that stern and graceful tribe usually spotted soaring in the sky or perched high in trees.

Also popular with winter and spring passengers is the Arts on Board program. Musicians, artists, and Native carvers,

In December young villagers don't miss out on Christmas: Santa Claus visits them via the Alaska Marine Highway.

weavers, and dancers journey on ferry runs and present frequent programs that can break up the monotony of a trip and enlighten visitors about the local arts scene. On one trip, Haines artist Donna Catotti might offer to sketch free portraits of passengers, while her husband Rob Goldberg paints a wildflower scene and answers questions. On another, Juneau's Bill Hudson might entertain kids with his amusing and fun diversions, while Clarissa Hudson explains the intricacies of Chilkat weaving. Entertainment is as diverse as the national touring company of Up With People singing pop songs, and the Juneau Tlingit Dancers sharing their traditional steps. Musicians might include jazz, country-western, classical, and folk singers.

During the holiday season, Santa Claus trades in his reindeer for more conventional transport on the ferry system. Bearing goodies, this sailing Santa visits towns and villages along Southeast's feeder lines. Youngsters flock aboard for a treat and the chance to deliver their Christmas lists in person. Ferry personnel, of course, take turns playing the big red guy. As with the arts and educational programs, the annual Christmas visit by Santa has become one more way the ferry system participates in life along the marine highways.

47

Handler Rebecca May lets Buddy, an adult bald eagle, stretch his wings on the back deck of the M/V **Matanuska.**

Conversations swirl and eddy throughout the ship as the M/V *LeConte* steams away from Auke Bay into the bright May morning. Nobody's in a rush. There's no way to hurry, and no particular reason for it, either. Might as well sit and chat for a while.

In the cafeteria, two white-haired Juneau women headed for retirement cabins in Tenakee argue mildly over state politics. Across the aisle, a pair of truck drivers play poker and review their strategy for unloading grocery vans in Hoonah. In the lounge, neighbors discuss Tenakee's dogs as if the animals were local personalities. "The best kind is the kind at Snyder's store," one man concludes. "Never any whining, doesn't bark or bite people," and his companion agrees with his estimation of the perfect dog.

Today's ports of call are not just Tenakee, Hoonah, Pelican, and Sitka. The true destination is the real Southeast Alaska, a place where few people live and still fewer visit. Out here, among tiny villages tucked away in inlets and coves and bays, you not only see Southeast Alaska—you're immersed in it.

On these feeder lines, the ferry becomes a floating town temporarily inhabited by traveling Alaskans. The difference between the busy tourist cruises and the local routes is palpable. No one's videotaping the scenery. Nobody's writing postcards. Worn blue jeans, flannel shirts, and the brown rubber boots known colloquially as "Southeast sneakers" are more evident than color-coordinated travel clothes. When one of the few tourists on board turns from the rail and shouts, "Hey, there are killer whales out here!" the Alaskans simply smile, and someone gently takes the deflated traveler aside to explain the difference between the six-foot Dall porpoises skipping alongside and thirty-foot orcas, commonly known as "killer whales."

For some, this trip is a quest for relaxation, a refuge from urban demands. A trio of Juneau residents bound for a weekend's soak at Tenakee Springs pretend to read their books as they recline gratefully under the warm sun, nibbling at crab dip and crackers. A woman skips rope on the solarium deck. Kids heckle a fisherman who has bared his feet. When a ship's engineer crosses the crowded deck and remarks, "It doesn't get any better than this, does it?" everyone nods and smiles. "You said it," someone answers. "Springtime in Alaska."

> Out here, among tiny villages tucked away in inlets and coves, you not only see Southeast Alaska—you're immersed in it.

49

◄ *In the waters of Lynn Canal, a humpback whale breaches off the stern of the M/V* LeConte.
▲ *Wooden beams of light halo the head of this totem pole figure in the Native village of Klawock.*

The M/V LeConte rounds a bend into the Native village of Hoonah, where the old Hoonah cannery can be seen on shore.

"Anchorage, Fairbanks—you can have 'em," says a Sitka man bound for Pelican. "Even Juneau's getting too big for me. I guess you could say me and cities don't mix."

Most people scattered among the islands of the Alexander Archipelago feel that way. For them, this is the sane way to live, cradled among mountains, guided by tides. It's a matter of philosophy: A person should live near the wilderness and work hard to reach civilization, not the other way around.

Southeasterners live on the continent's fringe, not just geographically but culturally. As remote as Ketchikan or Juneau can seem, communities still more isolated lie beyond them. Small towns may be the same everywhere, but transplant Smalltown, Kansas, to an island on the rim of the Pacific Ocean, and life is bound to take a few interesting turns. No pavement leads to the world. Bad weather can instantly shut out planes. The perks of civilization—hospitals, social and business services, instant entertainment—disappear. So do many of the problems.

The result is a kind of island attitude, concocted from one part self-reliance, one part easy-going spirit, and two parts connection, whether it's to family, community, or landscape. It's not a lifestyle; it's a life. If Southeast Alaskans don't gush over the scenery during ferry trips, it's not because they're jaded. Anyone who chooses to live on the outer edge feels a deep-rooted love for the land and wildlife that can't be expressed in a simple "Wow!"

All kinds of people live out here, many of them different facets of the same cut. Loggers and environmentalists agree to disagree about the role of the rain forest. Seiners, trollers, and gillnetters joust with each other until competition from sport anglers and charter boats prickles them into solidarity. Old-timers and

Traditional Tlingit totem poles stand in Klawock Totem Park on Prince of Wales Island.

51

newcomers try to shape their communities to their own particular visions. The closeness that ties communities together can also chafe. "You have to be careful what you say. You might offend someone you meet every day," says a Tenakee resident.

Out here, away from the crush of tourists, Alaskans are a low-keyed lot. Nobody has to impress anyone by posing as an old sourdough or brandishing an arsenal of bear stories. But there's a generous spirit among islanders, an openness to those who find their way beyond the tourist routes. Kids biking along Tenakee Avenue offer a friendly "Howdy-do" to strangers. A Klawock taxi driver detours to offer an impromptu tour through his village, pausing by canneries collapsing into history and the totem park where a score of graceful poles evoke an ancient aura. A truck driver who offers a stranded traveler a ride from the ferry terminal in Hollis to the small fishing community of Craig points out a new grocery store along the way. "Now I'll have four kinds of Raisin Bran to choose from," he jokes.

And so civilization presses on, even to Prince of Wales Island. The Klawock taxi driver notes that he left his home village to travel the world, living in San Francisco and Ketchikan along the way. "Now Klawock is getting too big," he says, shrugging. "Maybe I'll have to move to Coffman Cove. There's—what?— thirty people all told." Just about the right number of neighbors, to his way of thinking.

In the island labyrinth of the Alexander Archipelago, the marine highway system is not just convenient but critical to the region's seventy-thousand residents. Summer travelers often don't realize the important role ferries play in the social and economic life of Southeast Alaska. "We may get a lot of tourists, but these are not tourist ships," says steward Mary Cannon. "These are Alaska

The M/V LeConte docks at Tenakee Springs, a village on Chichagof Island famed for its natural hot springs.

53

A resident of Craig, a small fishing village on Prince of Wales Island, strolls down the town's boardwalk.

On Prince of Wales Island, local teenagers swoop across the face of the Thorne River on a rope swing.

ships. These are our highways. We have to run year-round."

Faster than barges, less expensive and more reliable than air service, ferries transport goods as well as people. However much the sea provides, it has yet to produce fresh milk. Many villages rely on ferries to deliver vanloads of groceries, surface mail, building materials, construction equipment, and other necessities. Stores from Ketchikan and Juneau sometimes send vans carrying pianos, televisions, stereos, business supplies, and other retail items on the rounds of small communities, a new wrinkle on the traveling salesman. Ferries charge by the foot, not the pound, making the vessels more economical for some suppliers.

It works both ways. Villagers head to Juneau, Ketchikan, and other large towns to shop, visit the doctor or dentist, see a movie. Petersburg residents call it "Kake Day," the day when the ferry delivers folks from the Native village on the other side of Kupreanof Island. During the fishing season, cold storages in some villages ship catches to the larger communities for processing and distribution.

Studies explain these economic connections in abstract terms, but it's possible to see how it works simply by watching people board and leave the ferries. Pickup trucks bound for Metlakatla arrive crammed with new fishing gear, dog food, even shrubs. Passengers struggle aboard with bulging shopping bags from Ketchikan's department stores. At Tenakee, a retired couple disembarks pushing a handcart loaded with boxes of groceries and flats of pansies. In Pelican, a huge bouquet of flowers bounces on the seat of the ferry's baggage cart, a special delivery for somebody. Cement trucks rumble off at Hoonah, drums already turning and ready to pour.

In winter, the ferries become even more important. The fog, rain, and wind that ground airplanes rarely stop ferries. In fact, the marine highway has rescued many travelers stranded in airports by the season's notoriously bad weather. "I never fly anywhere without my trusty ferry schedule," says a Petersburg woman who travels regularly throughout Southeast on business.

Ferries also serve as the biggest school buses in the world, carrying basketball, wrestling, and volleyball teams, bands, and classes taking field trips. Lounges and cafeterias serve as makeshift study halls and bedrooms. Thirty years of student travel has created a substantial body of folklore; many Southeast residents can recall with a grin or a wince various shipboard pranks. Some shenanigans have become legends, which means no one knows how true they are—whether a boys' basketball team really did throw a cigarette machine overboard, for example. One deckhand recalls hearing a recent horror story about a teenager who, prompted by a dare, inched around the ship's sponson, the ledge protruding around the hull just above sea level. The ferry system wields the ultimate disciplinary tool, though; schools that misbehave are banned from the ferries for the season, a punishment few school districts can afford. It works, says one purser thinking of a certain exiled school. "They come on now, they're very gracious."

Ferries are so popular during some annual events that schedules warn passengers to expect crowded runs. The Little Norway Festival in Petersburg, the Southeast Alaska State Fair in Haines, and the Gold Medal basketball tournament in Juneau often begin informally on the ferries, as old friends renew acquaintances and begin celebrating early. Potlatches, heritage celebrations, and other Native gatherings bring together villagers from the communities of Kake, Hoonah, Angoon, Metlakatla, Klawock, and Hydaburg.

All the rites of daily life occur on board as well. Babies have been born, marriages performed, friendships begun, romances sparked. One couple traveling to Pelican confess that they first met aboard the *LeConte*. Now married, they regard the ship as their own little love boat.

55

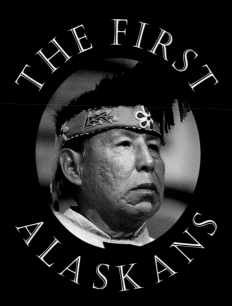

THE FIRST ALASKANS

Alaska's indigenous people, collectively known as Alaska Natives, take great pride in preserving their traditional songs and dances.

▲ *Tlingit elder Paul Jackson listens to a speaker at a Native gathering.* ▶ *The Thunderbirds perform at Celebration, a biannual gathering of Native dance groups in Juneau.*

Long before the Russians and other explorers arrived in the eighteenth century, Alaska was home to people who had learned to survive in a landscape that could be both harsh and beautiful. Today, these indigenous people are known collectively as Alaska Natives, but there are many cultural, linguistic, and geographic distinctions among them. The 1990 census counted nearly eighty-six thousand Alaska Natives, who represent almost 16 percent of the state's population. Most Natives live in rural areas.

The broadest way to distinguish Alaska Native groups is by area. Northern Eskimos, or Inupiat, live in four main groups along the Bering Straits, Kotzebue Sound, north coast, and interior north. Southern Eskimos, known as Yuit or Yup'ik, include those living on the Bering Sea and on the Gulf of Alaska. Athabascan Indians inhabit Interior Alaska in nine major groups between the southcentral coast and the Brooks Range. Aleuts occupy the Aleutian Islands and Alaska Peninsula. Tlingit Indians live in Southeast Alaska, as do small populations of Haida and Tsimshian Indians.

Each of these cultures is too complex and interesting to adequately summarize. However, travelers on the Alaska Marine Highway System will come in contact with Tlingit, Haida, and Aleut communities. In Southeast Alaska, modern Tlingits live diverse lifestyles, some in urban areas such as Juneau and Ketchikan, while others prefer village life in the more traditional communities of Kake, Angoon, Hoonah, and Klawock.

58

▲ *Pete Barrill, of Seattle's Ku-teeya Dance Group, dresses in traditional regalia for Celebration 94.*
▶▲ *As part of Celebration 94, Harriet Knudson from Hoonah plays the drum for the Mt. Fairweather Dancers.*

Tlingits far outnumber Haidas, who migrated north several hundred years ago from British Columbia to establish themselves on south Prince of Wales Island and on smaller islands. Hydaburg, the main Haida village, formed in 1911 when residents of smaller villages joined together. Newcomers to the region include Tsimshian migrants from British Columbia who moved to Annette Island in 1887 and founded Metlakatla under the leadership of Father William Duncan. A few years later, the island became a federal reservation.

As explained by anthropologist Wallace Olson, author of *The Tlingit*, both Haida and Tlingit society are matrilineal, which means ancestry is traced through the mother's side. These societies are organized into two *moieties*, one identified with the Raven crest and the other most commonly with the Eagle crest. Members of one moiety could only marry into the opposite moiety, a custom that has since relaxed. Within each moiety are *clans*, each named for a crest or emblem identified with an animal or mythical being. Members of the same clan might live in different places, or *kwaans*. Large families lived together in family houses, which also had names. Within clans there were also different social ranks of people, including an

upper class, commoners, and slaves. Although Europeans and Americans were fond of describing Tlingit chiefs, tribes, princesses, and so on, the social structure was much more complicated.

Also matrilineal, Aleuts traditionally seem to have organized into housegroups that looked to a senior or village leader. The sea supplied most of their needs. Historically, Aleuts were among the most exploited and abused by Westerners, first under the Russians and then under U.S. control as recently as World War II, when residents of several villages were evacuated and sent to internment camps in Southeast Alaska.

Modern society has introduced further layers of organization. Following the landmark Alaskan Native Claims Settlement Act of 1971, Alaska's Natives formed as shareholders into thirteen regional and approximately two hundred village corporations. Among issues still being debated are tribal sovereignty and subsistence rights for Natives.

Many opportunities exist for travelers to learn more about Alaska Native cultures. Most cities and villages have exhibits and museums focusing on the history, art, and culture of local Natives. Dance and theater groups also perform for visitors in Haines, Juneau, Ketchikan, Sitka, and some smaller towns.

The design on Rodney Worl's Chilkat blanket identifies him as a member of the Thunderbird clan.

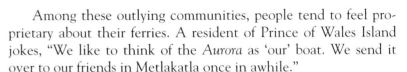

Among these outlying communities, people tend to feel proprietary about their ferries. A resident of Prince of Wales Island jokes, "We like to think of the *Aurora* as 'our' boat. We send it over to our friends in Metlakatla once in awhile."

The *Aurora* and *LeConte* are the workhorses of the Southeast fleet, faithfully making their rounds among the region's villages. In the summer season, the *Aurora* may make as many as thirty-seven ports in a week. The sole purser greets passengers at every stop, no matter what the hour, and off-shift deckhands are often roused to help handle lines and load vehicles. The overtime quickly accumulates, boosting paychecks and compensating somewhat for the chronic lack of sleep.

Some crew members consider the feeder lines boring, like "sailing around in circles," a deckhand remarks. Others who have spent years answering the same tourist questions over and over on the big ships regard these sailings as peaceful, homey. Locals are generally a calm, collected bunch who treat ferry commuting much as New Yorkers regard subway transportation. They know the drill: They board with a book, a pillow, a snack, and settle in for the ride. Grownups head for their favorite snoozing spot (the *LeConte* and *Aurora* do not have staterooms). Kids spread coloring books and crayons in the cafeteria. In small ports such as Pelican, Hollis and Metlakatla, the pursers take names, not money, from boarding passengers. Once the ship is underway, the pursers announce names over the loudspeaker, and the passengers know it's time to pay up.

These short runs produce an easy atmosphere not possible on the larger ships. In Pelican, where the summer's monthly ferry visit is a novelty, local kids—some of them the grown-up variety—wait until passengers disembark and then visit the

A commercial fishing boat, trolling for salmon on Cross Sound, passes underneath a rainbow.

Residents of Pelican sled their belongings down the town's boardwalk to load them on the ferry.

Perched on a rocky ledge in the Inian Islands, sea lions scan the horizon for possible intruders around their rookery.

cafeteria to buy ice cream cones. "That sort of thing probably wouldn't happen on the main lines," a purser remarks. Crewmembers often know their passengers after years of sharing the same trips. At Hoonah, a seaman idly casts a fishing line through the car deck opening and chats with a passenger as he waits for vehicles to board. No bites, but he's just killing time anyway. In the distance, a humpback whale breaches. "It's that Hoonah whale—always seems to hang out there," remarks the second mate. Even the animals become familiar.

People live their lives on board the ferry just as they would ashore. Black-cod fishermen headed to Sitka straddle lounge chairs in the *LeConte's* solarium and methodically tie new hooks to their long-line gear. A few thousand more, and they'll be ready for the 10-day opening. "All I can say is, we'd better catch some fish with these or else," one of them says, dropping another set into the box at his feet. As the ship cruises up Peril Strait, a couple of men forego the cafeteria's spaghetti lunch to share a slab of smoked salmon, and two young Hoonah women discuss the finer points of their halibut rods. Aboard the *Aurora*, Metlakatla schoolteachers on a weekend shopping excursion can't help but chat about the very work they're temporarily escaping.

On these runs, most dockings signify a homecoming. At Tenakee, a big goofy mutt leads the greeting party. Folks on the dock wave and shout hellos to folks on the ferry. "Absolutely charming," says a visiting California architect as she scans the tiny community's colorful waterfront. "It looks like you could run away from the world here." The dog sits attentively on the dock, tail wagging, as a gang of local men march aboard and carry off a shipment of lumber that will be used to rebuild homes lost in a major fire in 1993. The lumber's owner repays the amateur longshoremen with beer.

In Pelican, a happy tumult of dogs, kids on bikes, and townspeople with an hour to kill await the ferry's arrival for its monthly visit. A woman with "Grammy" marking her rubber boots leans over the railing and says, "I'm home! I'm home!" Born and raised here, she searches the waiting crowd for her brother and points out local landmarks to her companion. "I'm home," she says, hugging herself.

Even those passing through these ports have enough time to form attachments. A Juneau birdwatcher wanders to a nearby bluff not far from the Hoonah terminal and discovers two nesting kingfishers, their chatter echoing across the water. Others stroll through the small cemetery bordering the road, where rain-smoothed gravestones lie among beds of dandelions and forget-me-nots. Pelican passengers wash ashore like a tide, headed for burgers and beer at the town's two colorful saloons, or for a pleasant ramble along the lively boardwalk.

In 1976 when the *LeConte* began its monthly summer visits to Pelican, townspeople celebrated by closing schools, laying out a king crab feast, and holding a party that spilled into the ship's bar and lasted all the way back to Juneau. After all, the village's 160 residents had raised $17,000 to help pay for the dock's construction. But not everyone welcomed the ferry. Some saw it as a symbol of what they had wanted to leave behind. "It's the ugliest thing I've ever seen," one resident told a newspaper reporter. "Many people feel it's the first step in the wrong direction."

That's how life is in Southeast Alaska. For every yea, there's a nay. For every person yearning for more comforts of civilization, there's somebody else trying to escape them. Somehow, so far, the fulcrum of community delicately balances these struggles. The Alexander Archipelago remains a rural refuge, a coastal paradise, a place worth living.

Anyone looking for a good argument could debate the question: Which ferry route is the most beautiful? Certainly the main

▶ ▶ *Two kayakers paddling in Icy Strait enjoy a close encounter with a humpback whale.*

ferries cover more landscape on their runs. But the rural ferries seem to poke their bows into the extreme country, offering views where inlets are more intimate, mountains more imposing, wildlife more populous.

Sometimes wildlife viewing is like a symphony, small lyrical moments building to a powerful climax. No concert hall could be more stunning than Icy Strait, the marine boulevard that leads to Glacier Bay and Cross Sound. Many locals regard the passage to Pelican as the marine highway's most successful collaboration of scenery and wildlife.

The opening movement occurs with the gentle parabolic motion of harbor porpoises rolling through the water, displaying the small, tight beauty of a haiku. Suddenly, a group of Dall porpoises erupts from the water on a course toward the ship's bow, attracted by the waves. How do they move so fast? a passenger wonders aloud, and a man smiles and suggests, "Better design."

Near Point Adolphus, kitty-corner to the mouth of Glacier Bay, knowledgeable passengers scan the waters. Humpback whales returning to the bay's krill-rich waters often frequent this point. They do not disappoint today. A characteristic plume of breath and spume rises in the distance, followed by a second puff. Only small patches of the whales' broad backs are visible; it's easy to imagine acres of whale floating just below the surface. Moments later, broad tails wave like fans as the whales arch and sound in syncopation.

If this is a symphony, then the players have only been tuning up. The *LeConte* skirts Inian Island and emerges into Cross Sound, a portal to the Pacific Ocean. To the north, the broad tongue of Brady Glacier laps at Taylor Bay. The deep oceanic swell rocks the ship, and passengers crowding the bow brace their feet. Steady pounding and frequent furies of open ocean have rubbed the capes smooth. The bluff of Cape Spencer rises

66

On a bright summer day, a Sitka black-tailed deer pauses in its trek through the Tongass National Forest.

In the treetops overlooking Icy Strait, a bald eagle brings dinner home to a nestful of hungry chicks.

A mountain goat in the Tracy Arm-Fords Terror Wilderness ventures down to the tide line.

dramatically to the northwest. Beyond, the brilliant white incisors of the Fairweather Range pierce the blue sky, as astounding now as they were in 1741 when witnessed by Russian explorer Alexei Chirikov, the first European man to see this coast.

Cue the killer whales. A pair of orcas leap above the water, and for a moment the curved shapes, with their stark black-and-white patterns, evoke the image of the Tlingit crest design.

The ferry takes the scenic route toward Pelican, rounding Point Lavinia into Port Althorp, where Captain George Vancouver anchored two hundred years ago and sent out survey boats to chart the northern Panhandle. At one hundred feet, his war sloop *Discovery* reached less than half the size of the *LeConte*, which seems to suck in its gut as it squeezes through a narrow passage flushed with tidal action. Several harbor seals curiously raise their heads as they laze atop a seaweed-covered rock.

Inside the fjord-like reach of Lisianski Inlet, the occasional sea otter bobs belly up and calmly watches the ferry steam by. Fishing boats putter past, on their way to the deep blue sea from the sheltered haven of Pelican. A sea lion noses through the water, turning toward the few passengers who notice it. Attention is required; not every appearance of wildlife is bold.

On the return trip to Juneau, the *LeConte* eases into a timeless trinity of sky and ocean and land. The sun slides behind the mountains, leaving a brilliant orange sunset in its wake. A trio of humpbacks roll past the ship close enough to hear their deep, hollow breathing. A slivered moon rises.

And now the climax: As the ferry approaches Auke Bay, the northern lights glow and sputter, forming a double hook that reflects in the still water. Shards of green neon stab the darkness behind the Mendenhall Glacier. Passengers gather on the deck and gaze with heads back and mouths open. No one needs to say anything.

69

The northern lights flood the August night sky with waves of color above the spruce trees on Douglas Island.

The Alaska Railroad train rushes from the tunnel into a blast of light, and the scene is almost too much to take in: snow-thatched mountains, thick wedges of glacial ice that appear to be creeping into the town of Whittier, the M/V *Bartlett* docked in the crowded harbor. The fourteen-mile train ride from Portage to Whittier is the most novel prelude to a ferry ride on the Alaska Marine Highway System.

The train whistle shrills as it rocks to a stop, and drivers roll off the flatbed cars and onto the *Bartlett*, which waits with bow raised high and gaping open onto the car deck. This knighthead bow, so-called because of its resemblance to a knight's helmet, is the only one among the fleet's ships. Soon, the *Bartlett's* own horn echoes as the ship reverses away from the dock and sets off for Valdez. The 130 passengers aboard do not stretch the ship's capacity of 210, but the boat seems crowded as people colonize the forward lounge and pack solarium seats for an open-air view.

There is plenty to see in Prince William Sound. Imagine tugging on the ends of the Inside Passage until the coastal strip curves into a horseshoe. Montague and Hinchinbrook islands barricade the sound from the wild wind and waves washing in from the Gulf of Alaska. The bowl shelters deep fjords, a score of tidewater glaciers, and numerous islands. Mountain ranges crown the horizon. Chugach National Forest rings the coast. This irresistible combination draws many Alaskans from Fairbanks, Anchorage, and surrounding communities to sightsee, hike, fish, sail, camp, and beachcomb in their private paradise.

Practically speaking, the *Bartlett* offers residents of Whittier, Cordova, and Valdez an easy way to cross the sound. The Whittier-to-Valdez route links the state's two major highways, the Parks and the Richardson. For Cordova, isolated from the state's main road system, the ferry represents important access. But the scenery gilds the purpose. The *Bartlett's* summer schedule coincidentally provides popular one- or two-day tours of the sound—so popular, in fact, that crewmen tell about one trip so crowded that a passenger was reduced to tears in her search for a seat.

At other times, the ship is virtually deserted. Once a single passenger boarded for the trip between Cordova and Whittier. The crew overwhelmed him with attention: "We told him we'd buy his dinner, but he wouldn't eat it," a deckhand says. True to the marine highway's philosophy,

> **The irresistible combination of deep fjords, tidewater glaciers, and numerous islands draws many visitors as well as Alaskans.**

◀ *Passengers crowd the rail of the M/V* Bartlett *to see icebergs calved off the Columbia Glacier.*
▲ *Glorying in the sensation of wings over wind, a black-legged kittiwake soars high above the Alaska Peninsula.*

Crossing Prince William Sound on board the M/V Bartlett means having time to drink in the sunshine and scenery.

the ship sails no matter what. "We've got a schedule. We've got a ship. We've got a crew. Everybody understands this job has to get done," says Captain Walter Jackinsky, the *Bartlett's* master and senior captain of the fleet.

Nobody's thinking about logistics as the *Bartlett* crosses the placid waters of Passage Canal and Wells Passage into the sound. As the ship maneuvers close to a rookery of black-legged kittiwakes clinging to a bluff, the shrieking birds compete with a waterfall pouring into the sea. Fishermen in a seiner wave good-naturedly at passengers. Kayakers paddle along the green coast, turning their slender craft into the ship's wake.

In midafternoon, as the ship approaches Columbia Glacier, icebergs speckle the channel and line the beaches like an unstrung pearl necklace. The *Bartlett* enters Columbia Bay and creeps toward the massive glacier. Five miles wide at the face, rising three hundred feet into the air, the tidewater glacier is one of the state's most impressive natural wonders. The ice river extends forty-one miles from mountains to sea, but it has been receding rapidly since the early 1980s, spawning the crush of icebergs that prevents the *Bartlett* from approaching the face closer than a couple of miles. Passengers snuggle into their coats and watch as the *Bartlett's* pilot picks his course through icebergs the color of sky. The ship moves so slowly and carefully it's possible to hear the carbonated sizzle of ice releasing air. The sculptured bergs cast blue reflections on the water. Passengers are enchanted despite the glacier's chill breath.

"Oh, this is unbelievable," says a New Yorker. "I can't believe two days ago it was ninety-nine degrees."

"Enjoy the fresh air. This is as fresh as it comes," her husband says, drawing in a chestful. "Take a deep breath and take it home with you."

Photographers scramble to capture the image of two bald eagles soaring over the gently undulating field of ice. An Alaskan

73

One traveler uses a sleeping bag and a good book to shield herself from the frosty ocean breezes.

offers to snap photos of four friends posing against the glacial backdrop, and each of the men hands her his camera. One fellow jokes about how people back home will ask, "Did you see the glacier?" and he'll answer, "No, we were too busy taking pictures."

In the dining room, the third dinner seating enjoys the view of the glacier as an accompaniment to entrees of turkey and mashed potatoes, or fresh Copper River pink salmon steaks. When the ship slows and stops, nobody expects that anything more spectacular could appear until a pod of orcas erupts from the water. Three or four whales skim slowly along the surface off the stern; a few others circle near a seiner, competing for salmon. Two of the powerful whales approach the ferry so closely passengers can study the spray of gray speckles marking their backs. Finally, the wheelhouse announces apologetically that the ship must move on to Valdez.

The dinner show is not over yet, however. Several minutes later, the ship slows again as it passes a large green buoy painted No. 9. Five sea lions loll on the buoy's platform, barely bothering to glance at the ship. One of them unconcernedly scratches its sleek head with a leathery flipper.

At the head of Valdez Arm, the *Bartlett* waits for the oil supertanker *Keystone Canyon* to clear the constricted throat of Valdez Narrows. Once the gigantic tanker has eased past, the ferry slows again for seiners who have spread their nets across the channel to harvest a salmon run coursing below the surface. Prince William Sound provides some of the state's richest fishing grounds, and passengers lining the decks watch Alaskans working hard at one of the region's most important industries. As the ship picks its way among a score of boats and nets, it would be hard to say who is watching the ferry's progress more carefully—the fishermen or the ship's pilot.

The lights of the Alyeska pipeline terminal glitter across the bay as the *Bartlett* ties up in Valdez. Locals cast fishing lines from

Docked at Whittier, the M/V Bartlett raises its knighthead bow to allow cars and trucks to disembark.

Tankers pull into Valdez Terminal to load up with oil that has traveled down the trans-Alaska pipeline.

Fine private homes stand on Knob Hill, looking down on the waterfront town of Cordova.

the dock as the ship nearly empties. Valdez has weathered a lot of chaos over the years: the destruction of much of the original town during the 1964 earthquake, the subsequent move to this new townsite, the construction of the trans-Alaska pipeline, the *Exxon Valdez* oil spill in 1989. The peace of this summer evening reveals nothing of the community's tumultuous history, and when the ship casts off for the overnight journey to Cordova, almost no one will be awake to stare toward Bligh Reef, site of the catastrophic oil spill. Whatever effects remain of the spill, a deeply controversial matter in Alaska, they are not visible from the *Bartlett*.

A rosy sunrise and the tangled melodies of songbirds greets those few who are awake for the 4 a.m. arrival at Cordova. A lone backpacker leaves the ferry and trudges past the canneries and into the deserted town. Every town should be seen while asleep, with its character laid bare. Cordova's lifeblood is obvious; the harbors and waterfront are like another little city. Even at this hour, people stir on the docks as fishing boats glide in and out of the harbors, motors thrumming. The retired *Chilkat*, the state's first ferry, lies quietly at the dock, a Gulliver among Lilliputians. A sea otter floats on its back gnawing on a breakfast morsel as a seagull eyes the food.

Many of the *Bartlett's* crew live in Cordova when they're not living on board the ship. Unlike the week-on, week-off schedule in Southeast, Southwest crews compensate for a smaller pool of employees by working for as long they can stand it, the unofficial record being eighteen months without a break. That's seven days a week, working four hours on and eight off. Some crew members have spent more than half of their working lives on the *Bartlett*. Captain Jackinsky performed the wedding ceremony on board for a deckhand and his wife because the seaman couldn't leave the

Near Cordova, a bridge damaged in the 1964 earthquake crosses over the Copper River.

One couple admires the jagged edge of Childs Glacier in the Chugach National Forest.

ship. When Chief Officer James Soucie heads ashore on leave, he jokes, he doesn't even want to see a picture of the *Bartlett*.

Perhaps the *Bartlett* has a homey, comfortable feeling because people do live on it. The sign announcing hours for the dining room reads: "Breakfast, 7:30 a.m. 'til fed. Lunch, 12:00 'til fed. Dinner, 5:30 ' til fed." Unlike other ferries, passengers are allowed on the bridge wings; only a rope separates them from the wheelhouse crew. The message is: We do whatever it takes. "It's plain. It's a cattle boat. About the plainest ship in the system," says Boatswain Tom Faulkner. "But she's reliable."

With the kind of weather the Gulf of Alaska dishes out, plain but reliable is what you want in a ship. "The weather can be real good, and other times it can be really vicious," Captain Jackinsky says, recalling fifty-knot winds. Ordinary Seaman Larry Edwards describes water splashing over the rails, twenty-five-foot seas in the gulf, wind chills of forty below, and snow piling on the ship's decks.

And so the *Bartlett* makes her rounds, day after day, circling the minor sea of Prince William Sound. As the ship prepares to leave Cordova, Larry Edwards tosses scraps overboard to the terminal manager's small black dog, who snatches them from the air in what's become a regular ritual. "That dog will lose forty pounds when I'm gone," Edwards says, shaking his head. On the return trip to Whittier, a Cordova woman scans a fleet of gillnetters working near Esther Island for her husband's boat. "There he is," she exclaims, focusing her binoculars. In the front lounge, a crewman discusses his grandchildren with acquaintances on their way to Anchorage. Beneath the bustle of the tourist trade, the undertow of life among family and friends runs deep on the *Bartlett*.

The M/V *Tustumena* steams through a maritime Twilight Zone, where fog erases any distinction between sea and sky. Only puffins and murres skittering off into the mist betray the existence of the world. Throughout the night the ship's foghorn blasted every couple of minutes to warn boats not equipped with the *Tustumena's* sophisticated radar equipment. The mournful signal of a bell buoy peals somewhere to port; land must be near.

When vague shapes appear and resolve into Kodiak Island, passengers are relieved. Most have signed on for a week-long trip from Homer to Dutch Harbor and back. It's not a trip for everybody, but those on board want to see something new, something different. At the very least, they'd like to see *something*.

Among the 120 or so people aboard are citizens of Israel, Scotland, Sweden, Canada, and Germany, Alaskans visiting another realm of their state, and tourists who have visited Alaska before and now seek another geographical extreme. One passenger, a parochial school teacher from the Bronx, made this trip last year and has returned for another week of complete relaxation. An older Aleut man, now living in Kodiak, is making his first trip to Dutch Harbor since he was stationed there after the war.

"I'm totally and constantly amazed at the enthusiasm of tourists," remarks Captain Richard Seigel, master of the *Tustumena* for the past fourteen years. "These people are enthusiastic despite this being an odd vessel to be on. Even figuring out how to get out here is odd."

The *Tustumena* makes the journey between Homer and Dutch Harbor once a month from May through September. Winter weather is too extreme even for a 296-foot ocean-going ship equipped with stabilizing fins. Summer is no guarantee of a pleasant sailing, either; one trip might enjoy clear skies and calm seas, while another is encased in fog or plagued by ten-foot waves and thirty-knot winds. "You pretty much have to work around the weather or you might as well drag it on shore

Across Homer Spit and Kachemak Bay can be seen the pointed peaks of the Kenai Mountains.

and make a restaurant out of it," says Seigel of his ship.

Under these conditions, it's no wonder the ship is nicknamed the "Dramamine Express." Unlike other ferries, seasick bags are conveniently placed within reach of passengers. Velcro attaches family pictures to surfaces in Seigel's stateroom. Two of the lifeboats are fully enclosed vessels more suitable for open ocean than life rafts. "Now when the Fargo paper talks about weather in the Aleutians, I'll know what they mean," grumbles one passenger after a long night of churning through six- to eight-foot seas and deep swells that unsettled many stomachs.

Except for winter layups when the ship is out of service, the *Tustumena* makes regular rounds among Homer, Seldovia, Kodiak, Port Lions, and Seward. The trips between Homer and Seldovia, and Kodiak and Port Lions, are puddle-jumps compared with the longer stretches across open water from Homer and Seward to Kodiak. But even if there are only eight passengers and three cars, the "Trusty Tusty" sails. The ship also makes a special trip across the Gulf of Alaska each winter to carry state legislators, their staffs, and household goods from Seward to Juneau. Some of the crew grimace remembering one trip when terrible weather forced the ship back to Cordova and unhappy passengers seemed to blame the ferry system, as if the weather has ever been partisan.

As for the crewmembers, some find the Aleutian trip a diversion from their usual routine. For Captain Seigel, who went to sea when he was fifteen, sailing across the open ocean is, well, fun. Challenging. Others prefer sticking closer to their home ports. Mostly, the run along the Aleutian Chain is simply more time at sea for sailors who spend months on board before heading ashore for long leaves. ("Thirty-eight days to go," says a crewman. "But who's counting?") They spend so much time working together, in fact, that seamen tie up, unload the car deck, and rig the gangways with a fluid economy of motion and hardly any words.

A Kodiak resident participates in the town's Russian heritage by attending service at the Holy Resurrection Orthodox Church.

The *Tustumena* is a familiar sight in communities along the Kenai Peninsula. The Seward trip makes a scenic cruise along Kenai Fjords National Park. The ship joins the summer frenzy along Homer Spit, colonized each summer by tourists, cannery workers, and locals selling the opportunity to catch a halibut or sightsee in Kachemak Bay. The vessel's hour-long nip across the bay to Seldovia is a sedate diversion. And hardly anyone takes a second look at the ship as it docks for the afternoon in Kodiak.

But the monthly arrival of the *Tustumena* is a big event in the tiny communities along the Alaska Peninsula and in the Aleutians, where people spend their summers toiling in the fishing industry. The *Tustumena's* elevator loading system allows it to disgorge vehicles at the motley variety of docks it encounters along the way; cannery workers or state employees help with lines. "This is a tricky tie-up here," says a deckhand as she eyes the Chignik dock, which reportedly served as a bridge in an earlier life.

Cheerful chaos engulfs the dock as fishermen and townspeople gather to greet the ferry. Dogs mill around. Kids clamber off nearby fishing boats and onto the dock. The ship's cook gets off to buy fresh salmon for dinner. One woman disembarks saying, "I have to see if any bears are at my house," referring to the extralarge bruins that roam the Alaska Peninsula. Another advises those around her, "If you guys have hooks and lines you could go after pogies on the dock." She leaves, tenderly carrying a crate of spruce tree seedlings to start her own little forest.

Down on the car deck, townspeople display souvenirs and crafts as crew and passengers nibble on free samples of the kippered red salmon and fondle the fox, beaver, and otter fur moccasins and mitts. Even more exciting is the cry "Man

82

Two girls at the Kodiak ferry dock patiently wait to greet their disembarking friends.

With the M/V Tustumena *docked at Chignik, a pair of fishermen haul the heavy nets out of their purse seiner.*

Unalaska's Bunker Hill overlooks Dutch Harbor, one of the busiest fishing ports in America.

overboard on the stern!" A young man who just unloaded his new all-terrain vehicle from the ferry has plunged off the dock when the machine's throttle jammed. No harm done, though. The sheepish driver safely climbs a ladder to face plenty of ribbing, and a nearby fishing boat hauls in the bobbing four-wheeler. Leonard, a retired Texan who witnessed the incident, relates his version to other passengers, adding, "The first thing that kid did when he reached the dock was take out his comb and fix his hair!"

Subsequent dockings are less dramatic. The schedule is tight, but most stops offer passengers an hour or so to leave the ship and stroll through town. At King Cove, home to a huge Peter Pan fish processing plant, mountains of crab pots line the community's main road on the spit. Signs warn of the constant presence of brown bears. The shipboard naturalist mentions that last year, two bears loitered near the dock, one with a halibut hook stuck in its mouth. The captain advised passengers to take a cab into town. A local points out a lone spruce tree punctuating the windswept landscape and says, "If you cut that tree down you might as well get in a boat and start paddling."

Pastel-colored houses shelter residents of Cold Bay, mostly populated by employees of state and federal agencies. Fields of intense blue and purple lupine interrupt the relentless green. At False Pass, local kids and their parents visit the ship while passengers hop off to look over smoked salmon, beaded earrings, and photographs sold by residents from their pickups and vans. The dock dog here (there's at least one at every stop) is a golden retriever who greets everybody. A ramble through the homey fishing community of Sand Point, on Popof Island, rewards passengers who visit the town store in search of provisions and souvenirs. "The hats are free for tourists," the clerk tells surprised customers, who wear their "Aleutian Commercial Co." caps all the way back to the ship. Akutan, visited in the wee hours, remains a mystery to passengers, few of whom awoke for the stop.

85

Wildflowers and a white picket fence guard the entrance to Unalaska's Cathedral of the Holy Ascension.

At Unalaska, the ship pauses a few hours before turning back to Kodiak. The historic Aleut community is known to many only as "Dutch" after the booming international port of Dutch Harbor on nearby Amaknak Island. The waterfront scene explains the port's standing as one of the busiest on the West Coast, with seafood processing, shipping, bottomfishing, and marine services employing most of the town's 3,500 residents, as well as a large population of transient workers. Seiners steam by on their way to a herring opening, and an enormous Russian factory trawler anchors in the bay awaiting repairs. Skeletal cranes stack containers onto the 710-foot Sea-Land freighter *Kodiak*. Towers of crabpots, heaps of net, and miles of line are beached along the spit. "Out here you could catch every fish in the world," a passenger muses, looking over the action. "And they're trying to," someone replies. Indeed, Dutch Harbor consistently lands more tons of fish than any other fishing port in the nation.

Residents are just figuring out how to play the tourist game, and a small fleet of rental bicycles, vans, taxis, and a school bus offer tours to the *Tustumena's* passengers. Stops include the Holy Ascension Orthodox Cathedral, the cemetery, and the "eagle sanctuary," also known as the town dump. Bald eagles adorn the scenery everywhere, as they perch on roofs and crabpots and cling to bluffs. Pillboxes and other World War II relics dot backyards and slopes. Passing a sickly cluster of evergreen trees, a tour driver remarks, "They don't look too good this year. They call that our national forest." One lucky group sees something no one else did: the driver's house, where his wife laid out a repast of mushroom soup and smoked salmon.

Heading out of Dutch Harbor, the weather clears and the scenery becomes a dramatic revelation. Capes and bluffs thrust

hundreds of feet from the ocean's surface. Waves carry on the unceasing work of carving spires, caverns, and fingers of rock. Vegetation cloaks the blunt islands like a velvet glove on a stone fist. There is no green like the Aleutian green.

Captain Seigel diverts the ship slightly to cruise through Akutan Pass and past the Baby Islands, the farthest-east breeding area for the rare whiskered auklet. This unprepossessing bird's most interesting features are the tuft of feathers on their heads and the fact that birders travel from all over the world—some on the *Tustumena*—to the Aleutians simply to see it. "If we don't see one, we'll get our money back," a woman says, and the captain jokes, "Double your money."

Rafts of the dark birds do appear, but most passengers seem more excited by large oceanic swells that cause the ship's bow to rise and drop thrillingly. Later, a cruise by the Haystack and Whaleback islands affords passengers a view of basalt columns and grassy mounds that shelter twenty-six thousand seabirds. Thousands of tufted puffins circle in the air like bees about a hive. Sea lions snooze on the rocks below.

Much of the marine life along the trip is unique to these waters. Passengers spot fin whales and a sei whale, as well as the more-familiar humpbacks and orcas. Comical puffins windmill past, too fat to launch themselves from the sea's surface. Almost no one misses a floating flock of two thousand northern fulmars. The shipboard naturalist points out varieties of kittiwakes, guillemots, auklets, cormorants, and other birds colonizing the region.

Also tantalizing is the view of the foot of Shishaldin Volcano on Unimak Island, but the elegantly symmetrical volcano remains shrouded, as do other active volcanoes sometimes visible along the journey. The weather remains coy, with clouds and fog veiling and revealing scraps of scenery. Passengers step outside to gaze mutely at the bold promontory of Castle Cape. Silvery skeins of

waterfalls cascade from bleak plateaus. Out here on the edge of the Pacific Ocean, the elemental nature of sea, sky, and landscape somehow combine to make the whole greater than the sum of its parts.

The long trip also promotes an atmosphere of camaraderie among passengers and crew. "On this trip, you have more time getting to know more passengers," Captain Seigel says. By the end of the journey, one deckhand surveys the lounge, where people have turned tables into camping spots, and jokes, "These people are beginning to look like fixtures." There has been plenty of time to exchange the stories of each others' lives, to play dice, read books and outdated newspapers, and watch wildlife movies. "Camp Tustumena" is what a free-lance writer from Denali National Park calls the shared adventure. A Swedish woman traveling with her Canadian cousins admits she expected to be bored. Instead, she says, she was so busy talking and gawking that she never read a single book. "I had a hard time finishing a postcard," she admits. A few confess they found the trip a little too damp. "But why should I holler?" asks Leonard. "I left Texas because it was too hot and dry." And most would agree with Jeff, a college student from Houston who characterized his experience this way: "I set foot on the Aleutians. How many people get to do that?"

A traveler explores a defense installation abandoned on Unalaska Island after World War II.

In August 1948, an unusual vessel entered Tee Harbor, nineteen miles north of Juneau, and maneuvered close to the beach. Long, flat, and homely, the refitted naval vessel pushed up against the shore. The craft's bow opened, and two cars rolled off the deck and across the beach over planks held together with chicken wire. Driving the new black Buick was Ernest Gruening, governor of the Territory of Alaska. He and the driver of the gray coupe, Juneau attorney Simon Hellenthal, had boarded in Haines to become the first of millions of ferry passengers in Southeast Alaska.

The boat, the *Chilkoot*, was owned by three Haines residents who had purchased and refitted a war surplus LCT (landing craft-tank) vessel for ferry service and sailed it from Seattle up the Inside Passage. As an owner later recounted, the flat-bottomed vessel carried fourteen cars and twenty passengers on its 121-foot length. The *Chilkoot* did not resemble the sleek, efficient craft that would follow it, but it was based on the same concepts that have made the Alaska Marine Highway System successful. Beginning in the 1930s, several studies concluded that Southeast communities would benefit economically from

In the 1940s the *Chilkoot* connected the region's waterways as well as providing Alaska with a direct link to the rest of the world.

regular ferry service. Such a system would connect the region's waterways with its few roads, as well as provide Alaska with another direct link to the rest of the world. All agreed it would appeal to tourists.

Soon after its humble maiden voyage, the *Chilkoot* was regularly carting vehicles and people between Skagway, Haines, and Juneau. Unfortunately, although convenient, the *Chilkoot* was not prosperous. Owners Steve Homer, Raymond Gelotte, and Gustav Gelotte had hoped to supplement the summer passenger season with winter freighting to lumber camps, mines, and canneries, but Coast Guard restrictions limited the ferry's scope. When it appeared that the *Chilkoot* might go out of business, the Territory of Alaska bought the vessel in 1951 and operated it until its retirement in 1957. To replace it, the Territory bought the M/V *Chilkat*, a ninety-nine-foot ferry that carried fifteen cars and forty passengers.

The Territory continued studying the possibility of a marine highway, and a flurry of studies proposed various configurations of vessels and routes. At the time, some ideas seemed outlandish. The *Chilkat's* captain, David Gitkov, criticized many proposals that eventually became

89

◄ *The M/V Chilkat, the state's first ferry, now stays quietly tied up to the dock in Cordova.*
▲ *A refitted naval vessel, the Chilkoot was operated by the Territory of Alaska from 1951 until its retirement in 1957.*

important passenger features on the ships, including showers, coin-operated lockers, and reclining chairs. He also wondered whether tourists would be willing to travel as walk-on passengers, particularly given the early-morning schedules: "2:05 AM, 4:55 AM, and 1:55 AM sailings and arrivals are not very much of an inducement to tourist traffic. Very few people will deem it a pleasure to turn out at 3:00 AM, in the rain and dark, with baggage, and then sit for hours in a reclining chair," he wrote. Pleasurable, no; acceptable, yes, as it turned out.

Long-time mariners had even more serious criticism. It seemed nearly impossible that such large vessels could safely and reliably run through the complicated and dangerous waterways of Southeast Alaska on such a demanding schedule. "You'll be on the beach most of the time," they predicted.

The federal government transferred the *Chilkat* to Alaska as a statehood gift in 1959. A year later, voters approved an $18 million bond, the first of several large bond issues that helped finance new vessels, terminals, and vessel improvements. Construction of three ships began immediately in the Puget Sound Bridge & Dry Dock Company of Seattle, and the *Malaspina* arrived in Alaska on her maiden voyage on January 23, 1963. Painted blue, white, and gold, with the state flag's design of the Big Dipper decorating its stack, the ship was hailed at its christening by Governor William Egan as "a great step forward" for Alaska. This was the first passenger service Southeast Alaska had enjoyed since 1954. As with the present fleet, with the exception of the M/V *Bartlett,* the ferry was named after a glacier.

The stately ship's inaugural cruise between Seattle and Haines was more enthusiastic than efficient. As one Seattle reporter recalled, "Like most new ships, the *Malaspina* had her bugs. The worst was a shiver that would hit her as she approached her 18-knot service speed. Alaska Governor Bill Egan had his bug, too, and his shivers. Egan hacked his way north aboard the

Malaspina with fevers and chills that developed into walking—or would this be sailing—pneumonia." The ship also required quick engine repairs; a special delivery of parts arrived from San Francisco by floatplane. Accommodations were limited and no hot food was available, but when the *Malaspina* arrived at Ketchikan, hundreds of automobiles greeted her by lining the shore and aiming their headlights at the ship.

Sister ships *Matanuska* and *Taku* joined the *Malaspina* later that year to offer regular service between Prince Rupert and Skagway. (The *Taku* enjoyed the most exciting maiden voyage of the three "blue canoes," as they were soon dubbed: she struck an uncharted obstacle in the Wrangell Narrows.) The three ships shared the same basic design: 352 feet long, capable of carrying 500 passengers and 109 automobiles. Staterooms, food service, solariums, and lounges were designed to make the journey comfortable. In 1964, the M/V *Tustumena* began service in Southwest Alaska as the fleet's only vessel certified for open ocean travel.

Despite early doubts, the system proved so popular that it quickly exceeded initial projections of 46,000 passengers and 13,000 vehicles. In the first year, the ships carried 84,000 passengers and 16,000 vehicles. Some critics believed the system should be self-supporting rather than subsidized, but state officials pointed out that no highway system pays for itself. In fact, the marine highway system cost less to maintain per mile than standard roads in Alaska.

Residents appreciated the convenience and flexibility of the system, and tourists discovered that the marine highway had, as a *National Geographic* writer noted, "opened a new trail to the north." By motorhome, by tour bus, and by foot they came to see the scenery John Muir had extolled a century earlier. In its first dozen years of service, the *Matanuska* alone logged more a million miles and made a thousand trips carrying 850,000 passengers

altogether. The system's popularity quickly forced the fleet and service to expand, funded by more bonds approved by voters. The main route was extended to Seattle in 1967, and five more ships joined the fleet during the following decade.

The most notorious—and beautiful—addition was the *Wickersham*, a 363-foot Swedish cruise ship refitted for ferry service in 1968. The *Wickersham*, or "Wicky" as she was familiarly known, arrived with liabilities. Under the Jones Act, her foreign registry restricted her to the run between Prince Rupert and

Alaska. Also, she could not carry many vehicles, and parts were difficult to obtain. The *Wickersham's* career was so politically contentious that one wag commissioned a bumper sticker that said, "Watergate Hell, Remember the Wicky." So that the *Wickersham* could travel between Seattle and Alaska ports, the federal government issued a three-year waiver of the Jones Act while the M/V *Columbia* was commissioned and built. Many Alaskans grew attached to the *Wickersham* and pleaded with officials to keep the classy ship. As a Ketchikan reporter wrote, "The superferry

91

In 1970, a Canadian ferry rescued passengers of the M/V Taku after it ran aground outside Prince Rupert.

The purchase of the luxurious superferry Wickersham *turned into a legendary political fiasco.*

Wickersham is a floating palace compared with the seagoing motels that make up the rest of the fleet." Nevertheless, the ship eventually was sold to the Finnish government and reincarnated as the *Viking 6*.

The flagship *Columbia* arrived in 1974 with problems of her own. The fleet's largest and fastest at 418 feet and 21 knots, she could carry a thousand passengers. Her 9,200-horsepower diesel engines were the biggest American-design engines built in the country. But, as one newspaper editorial put it, "Instead of being Alaska's pride and joy, the new *Columbia* is having more troubles than the *Wickersham* ever did." From the time she was delivered three months late, design and mechanical problems frequently hobbled her to shipyards and drydock for repairs. Three months after her maiden voyage, the ferry struck an uncharted rock in Peril Strait west of Sitka. The vessel limped to Seattle with an 800-pound boulder jammed in the hull. Two years after her launching, she went into drydock for major repairs and the addition of a bow thruster, which vastly improved her steering and performance.

Meanwhile, demand on the ferry system forced the ships to stretch in more ways than one. The *Matanuska, Malaspina,* and *Tustumena* were each lengthened (or "jumboized," as officials called it) by slicing them in half, inserting fifty-six-foot sections, and welding the pieces back together. The renovations added more staterooms. The *Bartlett* entered service in 1969 with a distinctive knighthead bow that opens (like a knight's helmet) for loading and unloading vehicles. In 1974 and 1977, the state added the *LeConte* and *Aurora*, each 235 feet long and designed to operate on short runs among outlying communities.

Over the years various ferries have endured mishaps, scrapes, and close encounters with the shoreline. The *Taku* had only been sailing a few months when two curious Petersburg boys snuck into the ship's vacant wheelhouse as the ferry idled at the dock. When

93

▲▲ *Put into service in 1974, the M/V LeConte was designed to make short runs between small Alaska communities.*
▲ *An unusual vessel with a knighthead bow was christened the M/V Bartlett, then Alaska's newest ferry, in 1969.*

nudging the trees. Within a day the ship was refloated, and she limped to Seattle under her own power. She returned to service three weeks later. The only lingering effect of the *Taku's* misadventure was the joke about a new drink available in the bar—the "Taku on the Rocks."

As the system cruises through its fourth decade, the ferries have proven to be the safest transportation system in the state, establishing a remarkable record considering the challenges of weather and terrain. Over the years ferries have made many rescues, coming to the aid of fishing vessels, cruise ships, and pleasure boats that were sinking, adrift, or grounded. In October 1977, within three days the *Tustumena,* captained by Richard Hofstad, saved two people struggling in mountainous seas on the fishing boat *Wind Dance,* and then helped find another boat missing off the Barren Islands. The Coast Guard rescue coordinator in Kodiak radioed: "Regret getting you off your schedule so much these past few days. Am considering permission to paint Coast Guard racing stripes on your vessel." When the Norwegian cruise ship *Meteor* caught fire in 1971 in the Strait of Georgia about sixty miles northwest of Vancouver, the *Malaspina* took aboard sixty-six passengers and four crew members. Tragically, more than thirty *Meteor* crew members died in the fire.

Ferries have carried traveling zoos and carnivals, movie crews, and other unusual passengers. Once the *Malaspina* even turned back to rescue a three-year-old Airedale named Jack that had chewed its way out of its kennel and fallen overboard through a tie hole in the ship's stern. Crewmen not only launched a lifeboat to pull Jack from the cold waters but also rounded up hairdryers to dry him off.

Over the years, the ferry system has received many letters of praise from passengers impressed that "everything that was to be white WAS white," that the *Chilkat* once turned back for a latecomer, and that ferries added special runs to accommodate high

they fiddled with the controls, the ship surged forward, yanking part of the dock out, and breaking two seventy-five-foot steel counterbalance towers. A crewman reversed the ferry just before it ran aground. No one was hurt, but damage to the terminal interrupted service to Petersburg while repairs were made.

Probably the most serious incident occurred in 1970, when the *Taku* ran aground on a small island just outside of Prince Rupert. No one was injured in the midnight grounding, but almost half of the ship wedged among the rocks with her bow

In its heyday in 1965, the M/V Chilkat *survived many a wintry blast.*

school teams, hold inaugural parties, and offer locals inexpensive tours of Glacier Bay and other backyard wonders.

Ferry officials have fielded a wide variety of complaints over the years as well, from people concerned about everything from frightening birds with the ship's whistle to restrictions on livestock on the car dock. ("We have had requests for the movement of beef cattle, goats, and even mink," one beleaguered official wrote to an angry horse owner.) Visitors and residents alike protested the early practice of throwing garbage overboard. A twelve-year-old boy whose family owned a cabin on Admiralty Island complained about the unsightly mess and the unwelcome visitors: "Then the bears we've got come down on the beach and tear it to shreds and that makes it look twice as bad." In 1970, the system began installing trash compactors on board and ceased the practice.

One of the most creative complaints came from a Cordova fisherman who wrote that the *Bartlett's* wake had upset a lemon meringue pie on his boat. The fisherman submitted a bill for $8.18 that included the ingredients, baker's wages, and "clean-up time." Port Captain H.J. "Red" Lockert responded that the *Bartlett's* captain could not know whether fishing boats were rigged properly to deal with wake or wind. But he invited the fisherman to join Captain Richard Hofstad on board the *Bartlett* for a piece of pie and coffee: "I'm told we have a fine baker aboard that ship and as a neighbor perhaps you would accept a replacement pie from the *Bartlett* galley?"

A perpetual source of complaints is the frequency and timing of service to various ports. As Lockert once commented, "Each community wanted us to get there at eight in the morning and leave at five in the evening. That being impossible, we didn't make it, but we're still trying." Scheduling depends largely on tidal movement through critical passages, but complicating the effort are unexpected mechanical problems and maintenance layups that take vessels out of service periodically.

Like highways everywhere, the Alaska Marine Highway System struggles with budget cuts, increasing demands for service, and bureaucratic and labor issues. Faced with an aging fleet, administrators continually consider new ways to expand and improve service. Plans call for a new 380-foot ocean-going ship to replace the *Malaspina* in 1997. The new ferry will run on the main line for part of the year, and will also be able to cross the gulf and relieve the *Bartlett* or *Tustumena* during maintenance overhauls. With the lessons of the *Exxon Valdez* still fresh in Alaskans' minds, the new ship will be able to help with spills or other coastal emergencies.

The system's popularity continues growing, and wise travelers make reservations early in the year. In 1992, more than 420,000 people traveled on state ferries. In 1994, summer trips, traditionally the most crowded, were so full in Southeast Alaska that residents found it difficult to use their own ferries, and the system added additional runs to an already-busy schedule.

Since the *Chilkoot* first beached at Tee Harbor nearly a half-century ago, the ferry system has evolved into an important transportation and economic force for the entire state. About 950 employees work for the Alaska Marine Highway System (the number fluctuates with seasonal changes), making it one of Southeast's largest workforces. A 1991 study reported that for every dollar the state spends on the system, almost three dollars spill into the economy, creating hundreds of jobs. Traveling by ferry has become a major visitor attraction; passengers account for one of every eight tourist dollars spent in Alaska. Measured in almost every way, the Alaska Marine Highway System was an experiment that has evolved into a seagoing success story.

All historical photos courtesy of the Alaska Marine Highway System with the exceptions of page 89, photo courtesy of the Sheldon Jackson Museum in Haines, Alaska, and pages 92 and 94, photo courtesy of the Alaska State Library: Lockert Collection.

I t's just another day at the office. But what a day—blue sky, calm seas, and a panoramic view of Tenakee Inlet. In the wheelhouse of the M/V *LeConte*, Second Mate John McMahon, his eyes constantly scanning the waters, picks up the binoculars and peers through them. "There's a humpback," he says. He clicks on a mike and announces, "For the information of passengers, there's a whale breaching about a mile ahead, putting on a show for us."

Though the weather is fine and the passage serene and wide, McMahon doesn't take anything for granted. He moves over to the chart table and studies a marine chart marked with proven courses. "I try not to memorize all of it. I don't want to get cocky. Out here you don't want to get too complacent," McMahon says. Still, this trip is a cruise compared with some sailings. "We do have times thinking, 'What am I doing here?' The fishermen go home, cruise ships go home, and we're out here," he says. "Then you get days like this."

"This" can make up for a lot. Like sailors anywhere, ferry crews tell all kinds of stories about bad storms, long hours, and weeks away from families. But they have another kind of story as well, about remarkable things they've seen, about places they've been, about a second life on the water.

"I live underneath the water line, and you gotta know I couldn't sleep if I didn't trust them."

People who work on the ferries lead divided lives. On the Southeast runs, most work a week on, a week off, bisecting their months between the "beach," as they call it, and the boat. On board, most of them quarter the day into shifts, working six hours on, six hours off. It's not an especially easy life, not for them and not for their families. They miss softball games, graduations, birthdays. Divorce is common; one shift on the *LeConte* dubbed itself the "Achy-Breaky Watch" because three of its members were suffering through various stages of romantic strife.

Still, there are satisfactions. "When you work, you work. When you're at home, you're at home," one woman says. Crews often develop a camaraderie that reflects the way they rely on each other, and how much time they spend together. "It's a second family. I know more about them out here than their wives and families do," a deckhand says. After all, he adds, most people only see their families at night. That kind of closeness has produced an efficient gossip network. "You can't do anything out here without everybody hearing about it," confides a seaman. "If there's a shipboard romance, people in Bellingham will know about it within the week."

97

◄ *Passengers wait to board the M/V* Matanuska, *unaware of how much work it takes to make their trip possible.*
▲ *Basketball is a good way for the crew to pass time on long layovers.*

Ferry crews lead a split existence on board as well. Passengers usually only see them at work: preparing salads, vacuuming lounges, tying up lines, tidying staterooms. Crew members eat, sleep, and relax in a warren of living and working quarters secreted from public view. They share tiny, spare cabins—typically, two bunks, a sink, a desk, and two narrow vertical lockers. Boatswain Tom Faulkner of the M/V *Bartlett* repeats the crew's common refrain: "Prisoners have larger cells than we do. In fact, prisoners would riot if they had to live like this." Passengers are surprised to learn that most crew members sleep below the car deck, but the quarters provide the darkness workers need to sleep during their odd hours. The position of the crew quarters also is a testament to the skill of the officers, says an assistant purser: "I live underneath the water line, and you gotta know I couldn't sleep if I didn't trust them."

Off shift, workers try to catch up on their sleep and entertain themselves by watching videos, practicing musical instruments, playing cards, reading. Others work out in exercise rooms set up on car decks or other places. The *Malaspina's* workout room is located in the stack, in a space known as the *fidley*. Employees can ride exercycles in "Club Fid," as they refer to it, while watching the scenery pass by through an open door.

As with any job, some employees don't like the hours, the pay, the duties. Some days are better than others. But many seamen wouldn't work anywhere else. "As far as jobs in shipping, these jobs can't be beat," says Chief Mate Scott Macaulay.

Passengers also don't see the long work shifts or the years of training and experience. Officers study for their pilotage exams by memorizing passages on more than a score of charts, learning the water depths, reefs, traffic lanes, and navigational aids. After making numerous trips, keeping a log, and studying the charts, they draw sections of the route until they've qualified on the whole passage. "We, as officers, pick the course. The crew is really

As the ferry cruises through Wells Passage, a crewman takes a break alongside the ship's life raft containers.

steering these ships," says Captain Mark Sundt. "We're totally dependent on their help at the helm. It's a team sport."

A close look around the ship reveals just how many teams there are. The steward's department performs all the duties of a hotel and restaurant—cleaning, preparing and serving meals, assisting passengers. In the engine room, engineers and oilers tend the gleaming engines that operate twenty-four hours a day. In addition to taking shifts at the helm, seamen load vehicles and passengers, tie up and let go the vessels, and clean and maintain the decks. The pursers handle administrative and passenger services; state trooper and medical training prepare them for situations ranging from disarming passengers to treating accidents. Thus, the steward clearing away dishes also knows how to handle fire emergencies, launch a lifeboat, and perhaps perform emergency medical care. "It's not the same as shaking sheets on the beach," a purser points out.

Some jobs require more patience than others. Loading the car deck can be nerve-wracking for drivers of unwieldy motorhomes and trucks, and taxing for the deckhands who must arrange them. "It's like a big jigsaw puzzle," says Chief Mate Scott Macaulay, who jokes that one of the deck crew's theme songs is "To Load the Impossible Load."

Crew members face situations ranging from loading circuses to docking in high winds, but working with people presents some of the most interesting challenges. "It's just a small version of life out here," says Senior Assistant Purser Lynn Olson. Macaulay has taken a punch from a drunk in Hollis and surprised amorous couples in unusual places. Judy Denton, who works as a bartender and as crew messman, likes the way her job introduces her to all kinds: rowdy Alaskans, visitors thrilled about their Great Alaska Adventure, guys spending their last dollars to head north and find work. "They've always got a sad story to tell—all you can do is sit and listen to 'em," she says.

Catching stowaways is a constant game. A sign in the Petersburg terminal displays a picture of a jail cell with the message: "Please be advised, all you have to do is fail to purchase a ticket to your true destination to become automatically eligible to win a Grand Vacation including bed and breakfast, pay court costs, and pay the full price of a ticket anyway! Need not present a valid ticket to win! See Purser for details!"

The system employs proven strategies to roust freeloaders, but often stowaways give themselves away, usually by bragging. Once the *Taku* succumbed to mechanical difficulties and the ship stopped in Ketchikan to unload all the passengers before continuing on. The next morning two stowaways appeared and began strolling about the ship, oblivious to the fact that they were the only passengers. Crew members didn't have much trouble spotting them. Able Seaman John Sanchez tells about a twenty-year-old adventurer from New Mexico who attempted to board the *Matanuska* illegally by hiding on the baggage cart. A passenger glimpsed his feet sticking out, and his career as a stowaway quickly ended. After the ship lowered a boat to return the young man to the Bellingham dock, the crew found him so likeable that they took up a collection and sent him ashore with seventy dollars. Most others don't fare so well. The system now requires southbound passengers to show their tickets as they disembark in Bellingham; those who can't are marched off by the police.

There are lighter moments as well. On the main lines, crew members have heard every kind of tourist question, most more than once. "How high above sea level are we?" is a perennial query. (Answer: About nineteen feet, the height of the ship's deck above water.) "What type of currency do you use in Alaska?" (American, of course.) Lynn Olson says it's amazing but true that twice she's been asked, "How often do you use the depth charges on lifeboats to repel the whales?" A list posted at the Skagway terminal offers answers to the "17 most asked questions over and over again *[sic]*." Among them: "No. There are no phones on the ferry. It was tried but the lines would get tangled when the ships would pass."

Yet, passengers are usually more grateful than grating. Children's drawings of the ferry decorate the purser's office on the *Matanuska*. Crews receive thank-you letters, postcards, and photographs of themselves. "We're in so many videos. We're movie stars and don't even know it," steward Mary Cannon says.

And then there are the ships themselves. Crews like to say each ship has its own personality. They joke about nicknames earned over the years: the Clumsy *(Columbia)*, the Malfunction *(Matanuska)*, and so on. But there's affection beneath the jokes. "The ship is like a mother to you," says one officer. "It does everything for you. It feeds you. It rocks you to sleep. It's a nice comfortable feeling, knowing security."

Weather is the sailor's constant companion, and Alaska's coastal weather is the Jekyll and Hyde of climes. A sunny, smooth passage can turn into an ugly struggle against high winds, heaving seas, and freezing rain. Asked if he likes his job, Seaman Ichirow Sawa smiles and says, "Today I do. But this trip can be bad when the weather's real bad." Boatswain Larry Pearce adds, "It can teach you something new every winter." Not even these seasoned sailors are immune to seasickness. "You haven't been sick until you've been seasick," McMahon says. During violent weather, sometimes the only difference between crew members and passengers is that the crew are still on their feet. The first rule of thumb, says a bartender, is "Don't look panicky." For many passengers the ferry ride is their first sea voyage, and they depend on a confident crew.

Chief Purser Homer Sarber, who began with the system in 1964, remembers legendary storms wild enough to cause a lifeboat to blow away, or the bridge crew to shout over the wind, or an anchor to break loose. Once the *Malaspina* encountered seas so strong that the ship rolled sideways and vans on the car deck fell over, squashing a half-dozen cars. When the ship rolled upright again, so did the vans. Captains sometimes take shelter to avoid the worst weather, but usually that's for the comfort of passengers, not because the ships can't take it.

The flip side of bad weather is the job setting. Over and over crew members say, "It's always different. You never get tired of it, no matter how many times you make the trip." They often spend their breaks watching the scenery alongside the tourists. "After almost twenty years I'll still go out and look at whales," says Junior Assistant Purser Barb Greene-Pearson of her quest to take the perfect whale photograph. "I have hundreds of dollars of pictures of open ocean where I say, 'Trust me. There was a whale there.'"

Some encounters are more intimate. A purser with more than two decades with the system recalls the day when the ship approached a humpback whale lying motionless in the water. As he stood at the railing, the whale arched out of the water. "He was every bit as high as the deck. I don't ever expect to see that kind of thing again," he says.

Most of all, it's the daily presence of simple beauty that makes these jobs worthwhile. Not everyone can look out the window at work and watch mountains slide by, or whales leap from the sea, or the sun flood across the ocean at sunset. "The water—that's what does it for me," says *Taku* Steward Arletta Hjort, a Petersburg resident. "I love being out here. I would've been out here sooner if I'd known about it." Many ferry workers discovered that feeling a long time ago. Boatswain Larry Pearce, who has wanted to go to sea since he was three years old, worked on the *LeConte* when it made its first trip in 1974. "It never looks the same twice," he says twenty years later, his hands confident on the helm. "I would hate to have to trade it for an eight-hours-a-day desk job in Juneau."

A crew member shoots hoops on the car deck of the M/V Malaspina *during a long shore stay in Petersburg.*

USEFUL INFORMATION

The Alaska Marine Highway
totals about 3,700 miles of
regular routes. Sailing all of it
would be like sailing from
Seattle to New York City
and part way back.

▲ *An adult mountain goat surveys
his domain.* ▶ *Hiking up out of
Tongass National Forest, an explorer
approaches the alpine waterfall in
Granite Creek Basin.*

M/V AURORA
Entered service: 1977
Original cost: $7.7 million
Length: 235 feet
Beam: 57 feet
Draft: 13 feet
Service speed: 14.5 knots
Passenger capacity: 300
Vehicle capacity: 47

M/V BARTLETT
Entered service: 1969
Original cost: $3.2 million
Length: 193 feet
Beam: 53 feet
Draft: 13 feet

Service speed: 13.6 knots
Passenger capacity: 210
Vehicle capacity: 40

M/V COLUMBIA
Entered service: 1974
Original cost: $22 million
Length: 418 feet
Beam: 85 feet
Draft: 17 feet
Service speed: 17.3 knots
Passenger capacity: 970
Vehicle capacity: 180

M/V LECONTE
Entered service: 1974
Original cost: $5.6 million
Length: 235 feet
Beam: 57 feet
Draft: 13 feet
Service speed: 14.5 knots
Passenger capacity: 300
Vehicle capacity: 47

M/V MALASPINA
Entered service: 1963
Original cost: $5 million
Stretched: 1972
Length: 408 feet
Beam: 74 feet

Draft: 15 feet
Service speed: 16.5 knots
Passenger capacity: 774
Vehicle capacity: 120

M/V MATANUSKA
Entered service: 1963
Original cost: $5 million
Stretched: 1978
Length: 408 feet
Beam: 74 feet
Draft: 15 feet
Service speed: 16.5 knots
Passenger capacity: 746
Vehicle capacity: 120

M/V TAKU
Entered service: 1963
Original cost: $5 million
Length: 352 feet
Beam: 74 feet
Draft: 15 feet
Service speed: 16.5 knots
Passenger capacity: 496
Vehicle capacity: 105

M/V TUSTUMENA
Entered service: 1964
Original cost: $5.2 million
Stretched: 1969
Length: 296 feet
Beam: 59 feet

Draft: 15 feet
Service speed: 13.5 knots
Passenger capacity: 220
Vehicle capacity: 54

Statistics from Alaska Marine Highway System Master Plan, 1991, and Annual Traffic Volume Report, 1993, Alaska Department of Transportation and Public Facilities

A crisp winter day finds the M/V Malaspina gliding through Auke Bay, past the Chilkat Mountains.

Arctic Ocean

Barrow

Prudhoe Bay

Bering Sea

Nome

ARCTIC CIRCLE

Fairbanks

Bethel

Mt. McKinley

Anchorage

Whittier

Portage

Valdez

Seward

Cordova

Homer

Cook Inlet

Seldovia

Bristol Bay

Gulf of Alaska

Yakutat

Alaska Peninsula

Port Lions

Haines

Skagway

Kodiak

Hoonah

Juneau

Dutch Harbor

False Pass

Cold Bay

Kodiak Island

Pelican

Unalaska

Akutan

King Cove

Chignik

Tenakee Springs

Angoon

Sand Point

Sitka

Kake

Petersburg

Wrangell

Pacific Ocean

Hollis

Ketchikan

Metlakatla

Hyder

Stewart

Prince Rupert

ALASKA

Bellingham

Seattle

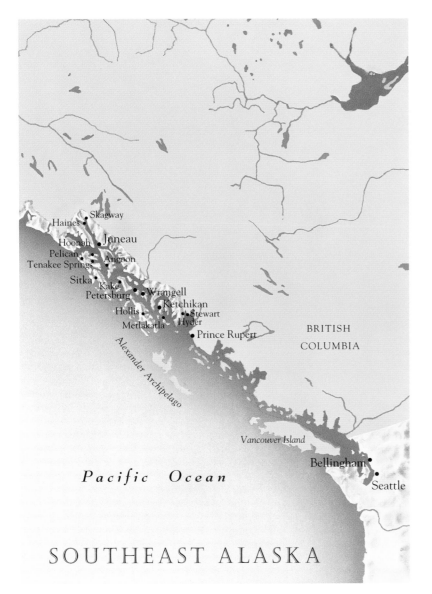

Skagway
Haines
Hoonah • Juneau
Pelican
Tenakee Springs • Angoon
Sitka
Kake
Petersburg • Wrangell
Hollis • Ketchikan
Metlakatla • Stewart
Hyder
• Prince Rupert

Alexander Archipelago

BRITISH
COLUMBIA

Pacific Ocean

Vancouver Island

Bellingham •
• Seattle

SOUTHEAST ALASKA

PORTS OF CALL
Southeast Alaska and the Inside Passage

ANGOON: This traditional Tlingit village of 700 is the only permanent community on Admiralty Island, most of which is designated wilderness. In fact, more bears live on the island (about 1,700) than people. Subsistence hunting and fishing, as well as commercial fishing, sustain much of the town. Sport anglers, hunters, and recreationists also base trips from here.

BELLINGHAM: About ninety minutes north of Seattle, Bellingham is the southern terminus of the Alaska Marine Highway System. The ferry terminal is located near the city's historic Fairhaven district.

HAINES: In this junction for the Alaska Marine Highway and the Haines Highway, the 2,500 residents depend largely on fishing and a growing tourism industry. The Alaska Chilkat Bald Eagle Preserve, about seventeen miles north of town, draws more than three thousand bald eagles in November and December.

HOLLIS: This tiny community of just over 100 serves as the ferry terminal for Prince of Wales Island and the portal to the island's 4,500 residents. A thirty-one-mile paved road connects Hollis with the Native village of Klawock and the fishing and logging town of Craig on the island's west side. Logging roads connect Thorne Bay, Hydaburg, and Coffman Cove to the main road, as well as several smaller towns and logging camps.

HOONAH: Fishing, logging, and a subsistence lifestyle contribute to this community of 800, most of whom are Native. Located on northeast Chichagof Island across Icy Strait from Glacier Bay, it is also popular with recreational boaters, hunters, and anglers.

HYDER: Fewer than 100 folks populate this quiet mining town at the head of Portland Canal. Two miles down the road at the Alaska-Canada border is Stewart, B.C. The road connecting these two communities leads about forty miles to the Cassiar Highway. The ferry visits Hyder weekly during summers only.

JUNEAU: Alaska's capital, Juneau is the state's third-largest city with more than 28,000 residents. State and federal government employ the largest percentage of workers, but tourism is highly important, with more than 350,000 cruise ship passengers visiting each summer. The city also acts as a commercial center for rural communities. The Mendenhall Glacier, about twelve miles northwest of town, is one of the state's top visitor attractions.

KAKE: A Tlingit town on northwestern Kupreanof Island, Kake has 800 residents who depend on fishing, logging, and subsistence. Visitor attractions include sportfishing, hunting, a historic cannery, and a 132.5-foot totem pole carved in 1967.

KETCHIKAN: The fourth-largest city in Alaska with about 14,000 residents in the area, this town relies on commercial fishing, tourism, and the Ketchikan Pulp Company for jobs. A few miles away, nearly four hundred people live in the Tlingit village of Saxman.

METLAKATLA: Founded in the 1880s on Annette Island by Tsimshian Indians who migrated north from British Columbia, this community of about 1,500 lies within a federal reservation. Livelihoods revolve around fishing and subsistence living.

PELICAN: This boardwalk community of 300 or so is tucked near the head of Lisianski Inlet on northwest Chichagof Island. Founded by Finnish immigrant Kalle (Charlie) Raatikianen, who named it after his fish packer, the *Pelican*, the colorful town's lifeblood remains fishing.

PETERSBURG: Settled as a Norwegian fishing village at the turn of the century, this town of 3,600 remains true to its heritage by thriving on fishing and seafood processing. Still inhabited by many families of Norwegian descent, the community invites everyone to celebrate its origins each May with the Little Norway Festival. Just over a score of residents live in Kupreanof, a second-class incorporated city just across the Wrangell Narrows on Kupreanof Island.

PRINCE RUPERT, B.C.: This port city of about 14,500 offers one of three road links to Southeast Alaska. Highway 16 from Prince George and the Canadian National Railway connect with Alaska Marine Highway and British Columbia Ferry System. Fishing, timber processing, and tourism bolster the town's marine shipping industry.

SITKA: Once the capital of Russian America, this fishing community of about 8,500 is famed for its lovely setting and rich history. Examples of its Tlingit and Russian heritage include the Sitka National Historical Park, St. Michael's Russian Orthodox Cathedral, Sheldon Jackson Museum, and the restored Bishop's House.

SKAGWAY: Once the staging ground for thousands of gold-crazed Klondikers, this town of about 700 each year welcomes even more visitors interested in its colorful history. The National Park Service and local merchants have restored many of the town's historic buildings to their former glory. Attractions include retracing historic footsteps of goldseekers on the Chilkoot Pass Trail and the White Pass and Yukon Railway.

TENAKEE SPRINGS: A wide path is the only avenue through this picturesque community of about 100 located on Chichagof Island. Miners once spent their winters soaking in the hot springs. Modern residents and vacationers still rely on the rustic bathhouse for warm water. The only transportation within town is biking, walking, or riding all-terrain vehicles.

WRANGELL: Four cultures—Tlingit, Russian, British, and American—appreciated this community's location near the mouth of the Stikine River, a major waterway originating in Canada. A sawmill, commercial fishing, and tourism support the population of about 2,600.

Hammer Slough rises and falls silently underneath the houses of Petersburg on Mitkof Island.

PORTS OF CALL
Southcentral Alaska

Yukon River

Fairbanks

HIGHWAY

*Denali
National Park
and Preserve*

PARKS

RICHARDSON HIGHWAY

ALASKA HIGHWAY

Anchorage

Whittier
Portage
Kenai Peninsula
Seward
Homer
Seldovia

Valdez
Cordova
*Prince
William
Sound*

HAINES HWY

Yakutat
Haines

Cook Inlet

Gulf of Alaska

Kodiak Island

Pacific   Ocean

SOUTHCENTRAL ALASKA

CORDOVA: Most of Prince William Sound's fishermen work out of this port, which also depends on processing to support the economy. Located on the mainland on the sound's east, the town has 2,500 residents who are isolated from the state's road system, although a proposal to open the Copper River Highway has stirred up bitter controversy. The nearby Copper River Delta and Chugach National Forest attract birdwatchers and hikers, as well as the boaters and anglers drawn to the sound.

HOMER: On the tip of the Kenai Peninsula, Homer draws sport anglers and commercial fishermen in search of halibut and salmon, and artists in search of inspiration. Nearly 5,000 people live in this town overlooking Kachemak Bay and Cook Inlet. During summer the Homer Spit is crowded with vacationers, cannery workers, and charter and commercial fishing fleets.

SELDOVIA: The charm of this reclusive fishing village, on Kenai Peninsula across Kachemak Bay from Homer, attracts visitors by ferry, plane, and water taxi to what was once a thriving fishing center. Today only about 400 people live in this historic waterfront town. St. Nicholas Russian Orthodox Church evokes the town's Russian past.

SEWARD: Located on southeast Kenai Peninsula at the head of Resurrection Bay, the town has a deep-water port that makes it ideal for cruise ships and freighters, while its link to the Alaska Railroad and Seward Highway make it accessible to the rest of Alaska. Sport and commercial fishing also contribute to the livelihood of the town's nearly 3,000 residents, as do tourists interested in the natural wonders of nearby Kenai Fjords National Park.

VALDEZ: Once Alaska's gateway into the Interior, Valdez is the terminus of the trans-Alaska pipeline, a major shipping port for oil tankers and freighters, a commercial fishing port, the beginning of the Richardson Highway, and a recreation base of Prince William Sound. About 4,000 people live here.

WHITTIER: Fewer than 300 people live in this transportation hub at the head of Passage Canal. The Alaska Railroad, the Alaska Marine Highway, the Small Boat Harbor, and the Hydra Train all use this deep-water port to transport people and goods between Prince William Sound and Anchorage.

Nome

Norton Sound

Fairbanks

Bering Sea

Bristol Bay

Anchorage

Cook Inlet

Seward

Homer

Seldovia

Alaska Peninsula

Shelikof Strait

Port Lions

Kodiak

Kodiak Island

False Pass

Cold Bay

Chignik

Dutch Harbor

Akutan

King Cove

Sand Point

Unalaska

Aleutian Islands

Pacific Ocean

SOUTHWEST ALASKA

PORTS OF CALL
Southwest Alaska and the Aleutians

AKUTAN: About 600 villagers live in this fishing community on east Akutan Island. Akutan Volcano, 4,275 feet high, is one of the most active volcanoes in the Aleutian Chain, with eruptions as recently as 1992.

CHIGNIK: A fishing village on the Alaska Peninsula, Chignik's population of 180 expands during the summer by several hundred fishermen and cannery workers. Nearby Aleut communities include Chignik Lagoon and Chignik Lake.

COLD BAY: Originally a World War II military base from which assaults on the Japanese invaders were launched, Cold Bay's claim to fame is its 10,400-foot runway. Employees of several state and federal agencies comprise most of the town's 150 residents. The community is located on the edge of Izembek National Wildlife Refuge.

FALSE PASS: This Aleut fishing village of about seventy is located on the east side of Unimak Island, where it grew in the early years of the century around a salmon cannery.

KING COVE: Settled by fishermen in 1911 and populated by Aleuts from other villages, King Cove's current population of about 700 centers around fishing and the large Peter Pan cannery.

KODIAK: With 15,000 people in the area, Kodiak is one of the largest fishing ports in the country. A U.S. Coast Guard base, fish processing, and a cargo industry contribute to the maritime economy. Also located on the island (the second largest in the country) are six villages and the Kodiak National Wildlife Refuge, which protects the area's large brown bears.

PORT LIONS: Just over 200 people live in this fishing village settled in 1964 by residents of Afognak, one of several communities destroyed in the earthquake. The townspeople named the community to thank the Lions International organization for its help in the resettlement to the north coast of Kodiak Island.

SAND POINT: Located on Popof Island in the Shumagin Islands, the 1,000 or so residents are largely engaged in fishing, fish processing, and marine services.

UNALASKA/DUTCH HARBOR: Unalaska is the name of the Aleut community located on the island of Unalaska, while Dutch Harbor is the international fishing port located on nearby Amaknak Island. Commercial fishing and processing have made this the boomtown of the Aleutians, employing nearly all of the 3,500 permanent residents and thousands more transient workers. More tourists are finding their way here, attracted by growing visitor services, birdwatching opportunities, and the area's Aleut, Russian, and World War II history.

On board the M/V Columbia, a passenger takes in the scenery along the Lynn Canal on her way to Haines.

In the twilight waters of Lynn Canal, the M/V Matanuska sails off into a golden sunset.